Add a new jewel to the king's crown!

Unless you've spent your life in a time capsule or a Manchurian monastery, you're familiar with Henny Youngman and his unique humor. The very mention of his name evokes a smile, and who is there who hasn't by now heard his classic one-liner: "Take my wife—*please*!"

Apart from being a genuinely funny man, Henny Youngman has a refreshing curiosity about everything in the world, and an exquisite faculty for putting his finger on the heart of the ridiculous. It is, therefore, a natural extension of his wit to find that he's up to the chin-rest of his violin in puzzles, riddles, party tricks, and "gotchas."

Here are some samples of Henny's off-beat, humorous quickie quizzes, which, on second look, are a little more subtle than they appear on first look:

Q: *I am something that every living person has seen, but no one will ever see me again. What am I?*
A: Yesterday.

Q: *What is it that Adam didn't have, yet gave to his wife? To his children?*
A: (1) A husband.　　(2) A father.

It's a show-biz axiom that comedians always want to play Hamlet. Not so with Henny Youngman. He simply wants to make people laugh—with the spoken word, the printed word, or the prank. And how he does!

WRITE FOR OUR FREE CATALOG

If there is a Pinnacle Book you want—and you cannot find it locally—it is available from us simply by sending the title and price plus 25¢ to cover mailing and handling costs to:

PINNACLE—Book Mailing Service
P.O. Box 1050
Rockville Centre, N.Y. 11571

____Check here if you want to receive our catalog regularly.

Henny Youngman's BIG BLUE BAMBOOZLE

PINNACLE BOOKS • LOS ANGELES

HENNY YOUNGMAN'S BIG
BLUE BAMBOOZLE

Copyright © 1978 by Henny Youngman

All rights reserved, including the right to reproduce this book or portions thereof in any form.

An original Pinnacle Books edition, published for the first time anywhere.

First printing, August 1978

ISBN: 0-523-40349-6

Cover illustration by Larry Noble

Printed in the United States of America

PINNACLE BOOKS, INC.
2029 Century Park East
Los Angeles, California 90067

Henny Youngman's BIG BLUE BAMBOOZLE

CONTENTS

Preface
Introduction
1. Jokes, Gags, and Teasers   3
2. Word Play   23
3. Stunts—Physical and Psychological   33
4. Tongue Twisters—To Be Read Only When Sober   63
5. Wagers with Coins and Bills and Other Money Betchas   75
6. Bar Betchas—Using Straws, Glasses, Drinks, and Money   97
7. Magic—With Cards, Cups, Cigarettes, Coins, and Matches   113
8. Mathematics—Betchas Using Numbers   125
9. Betcha Riddles and Conundrums   139
10. Oddities and Novelties—Betchas Using Everyday Articles   183

To Jenny & Jessica Leary

PREFACE

These one-liner gags and betchas have been carefully screened and tailored to give you, the reader, the opportunity of "victimizing" your host, your friends, and your relatives, and making them like it, through one-liner humorous challenges and gags.

These quickies are almost limitless in scope, as they can be adapted to almost any situation. They include betchas for barrooms, parties, and conventions, most of which contain built-in gags. There are many utilizing everyday articles such as cigarettes, coins, bills, and cards. There are some brain teasers and educational betchas employing mathematics, and still others that are magical, or unusual novel tongue twisters, and riddles—but all are designed to entertain and provoke laughter and even earn you a few shekels from the unwary who dare to betcha.

My sincere thanks to my dear friends Morty Rudnick (magician) and Professor Abe Hurwitz (Shari Lewis's poppa) for their invaluable contribution and aid in helping me to write this book.

—Henny

INTRODUCTION

Henny Youngman—dubbed "King of the One-Liners" by another headliner of yesteryear, Walter Winchell—is a living legend.

At seventy-one years of age, this man is a virtual dynamo, whose travels take him to at least four states each week, where he works conventions, theaters, condominiums, industrial shows, radio, television, and motion pictures.

His humor touches and titillates everyone from eight to eighty-eight. He knows what's funny; his stories and vignettes are funny but always in good taste. His timing is perfect and his delivery, rapidfire. It's no problem for him to be on stage for as long as he wants and to draw from his almost limitless arsenal of gags and humor.

But, for the sake of space and time, suffice it to say that Henny has entertained presidents, royalty, fellow comedians, many of the greatest who have come and gone, as well as millions of people the world over. Yet, he is still in there, greater than ever, making people happy as they forget their problems at least for the moments that he graces their lives with his humor.

It is indeed difficult to put in so few words the accolades to this great humorist and human being, so I can only sum it up in the words of another of his peers—his dear friend and comedian, the First M.C. of the late, great TV Broadway Open House, Jerry Lester: "He's a prince among men."

Amen

—Morty Rudnick
(close friend and admirer)

Glasses, straws, cigarettes, ashes, coins, bills, matches, and other things around the bar or table can be used to enliven the party and heighten the spirits. Here are a few select ideas that can make you the center of attraction as a natural entertainer, as you don't use any store-bought gadgets or gimmicks or seeming preparations.

If you are the kind who is made happy by making others happy, then these stunts are for you. Go to it; find an appreciative bar-side companion or two and have fun.

The following are challenges and guaranteed ice breakers that I have gathered through the years. They are separated into their special categories for the special occasions and to make the patter fit the occasion.

One-liners, or two-liners, or as many liners as the case may be, it was my intention to keep them short, concise, and to the point. All too often a good joke or gag has lost its flavor and interest because the teller dragged it out. In the following pages you will find these betchas and gags cut down and tailored in as few words as possible so as to give the greatest impact as possible, and thereby get the most entertainment from them.

Warning ... do these mainly with your friends or family or at the dinner table, between courses, and I betcha you'll enjoy your dinner and so will the family.

Henny Youngman's BIG BLUE BAMBOOZLE

1
Jokes, Gags, and Teasers

Where was the Declaration of Independence signed?

    At the bottom of the paper.

Why do they bury a man on the side of a hill?

    Because he's dead.

What does a cat have that no other animal can have?

    Kittens.

How many dead people in a cemetery?

    All of them.

What is the best way to raise vegetables?

    With a knife and fork.

If you are driving a taxi with five people in it, and at the first stop two get on, and one gets off, at the next stop three people get on and one gets off, and on the last stop three get off and one gets on—what is the driver's name?

"If you are driving," etc. etc.

What things can you never eat at breakfast?

Dinner and supper.

Why does a fireman wear red suspenders?

To hold his pants up.

What's the main qualification for having a military funeral?

You must be dead.

Why does a chicken cross the street?

To reach the other side.

Bet someone you can tell him the score of a game before the game begins.

Before the game, the score is 0–0.

Bet anyone that he has a hole in his sock. If he protests, ask him how he put his feet in his sock if he doesn't have a hole in it.

JOKES, GAGS, AND TEASERS

If a plane flying over the border of France and Italy crashes, where do you bury the survivors?

One does not bury survivors.

Can you put "yourself" through a keyhole?

Write the word *yourself* on a piece of paper and pass it through the keyhole.

I bet I can prove that I'm not a liar even though I say I am.

"I am a liar";
if you believe me, then I'm not a liar.
If you don't believe me, then I'm telling the truth;
then I'm not a liar.

What is it that Adam didn't have, yet gave it to his wife? To his children?

(1) A husband.
(2) A father.

How long are a man's legs?

Just long enough to reach the ground.

If herring costs seventeen cents a pound, what will a boat with herring come to?

The Jock.

Can a man marry his widow's sister in the United States?

To marry his widow's sister, he would have to be dead.

JOKES, GAGS, AND TEASERS

Can you show something to your friends that they have never seen before and will never see again?

> Yes. Take a peanut and crack it. They have never seen the nut that is inside that particular shell. Eat the nut and they will never see it again.

In Peru, if they can grow bananas three-quarters of the year because it rains, can they grow apples for the other four months?

> No, because there are only three months left.

Do you know anyone with all his fingers on one hand?

> No, each of us usually has five on one hand and five on the other.

Bet your friend that he can't take his tongue in his hand and touch his ear, while you can.

> Take your tongue in one hand and place your other hand on your ear.

Bet your friend that you can tell what is on any piece of paper. Tell him to write whatever he wants on a piece of paper and place it under his foot, and tell him what is on the paper.

> His foot.

A man leaving a restaurant wrote the following numbers on a piece of paper that he handed to the cashier. Can you figure out the message if these were the numbers? 1 0 2 0 0 4 1 8 0.

> I ought to owe nothing for I ate nothing.

If there is a gas jet, a candle, and a kerosene lamp and you only have one match to light them all, which should you light first?

> The match.

How far can a dog run into the woods?

> Only halfway; the other half of the way he would be running out of the woods.

What is it that a man can never have but can give to a lady?

> A husband.

JOKES, GAGS, AND TEASERS

How many birthdays does the average man have? Wanna bet?

One.

Bet you don't know how many species Moses had aboard the ark.

Moses wasn't aboard the Ark.

Say to someone that you haven't seen lately: "Betcha that I saw you yesterday."

That *eye* saw, etc.

The world is round. If I dug a hole through the earth at this spot, I bet that you don't know where you'd come out.

You'd come out of the hole.

Betcha I can ask a question that I could answer. And you can ask a question and you couldn't answer it. *Question*: Why doesn't a rabbit leave any dirt around a hole when he digs? *Answer*: Because he digs from below the hole. When the poor soul asks you, "How did the rabbit get into the hole in the first place?" tell him: "That's your question, you answer it."

A bus picked up four people, then three, then left off two ... bet you can't tell me how were were left on the bus.

> Six—remember, it had a driver, too.

Bet I can jump higher than the table.

> Of course. The table can't jump.

Betcha I can understand any language but Greek.

> When a foreign language is spoken, say: "That's Greek to me."

I put a picture of a piece of cheese in a mousetrap. Betcha you don't know what I caught.

> A picture of a mouse.

Bet a youngster that he doesn't know why he goes to bed.

> Because the bed doesn't come to him.

Kiss a book inside and outside without opening the book—this apparently impossible feat may be accomplished by kissing the book inside the room and then carrying it outside of the room and kissing it there.

JOKES, GAGS, AND TEASERS

I betcha I can name a large animal that you all know has four legs and flies.

> A horse.

I betcha you don't know who's in the hospital.

> Sick people.

Bet a bachelor friend that you know what his future wife's name will be.

> It will be Mrs.—(whatever the bachelor's last name is).

Make a bet with a youngster that his left shoe is on his right foot. When he checks and then takes you up on it, explain to him that his left shoe is certainly not on his right foot in the sense that "right" is the opposite of left; but that is is on the right foot because it is on the correct foot.

Betcha you don't know what a dog can do on three legs that a woman can do sitting down.

> Shake hands.

BIG BLUE BAMBOOZLE

Which would you rather: look a greater fool than you are—or, be a greater fool than you look?

> That's impossible!

Take out a piece of gum and ask: "Do you chew gum?" As the person extends his hand to get it, pull back and say: "It's bad for your teeth."

At a party of thirty people, bet that at least two people have exactly the same birthday—day and month.

I betcha I can prove I'm not here. "I'm not in Miami"; "I'm not in Memphis"; and, "I'm not in Chicago."

> Spectator: "No." (To all questions.)
> "I must be somewhere else."
> "If I'm somewhere else, I'm not here. If I'm not here, I win."
> (P.S.—If you're not here, then how can I pay you?)

I betcha I can make you say "no." "Oh, you must know this trick."

> Spectator: "*No*, I don't." Or: "How do you pronounce n-o?"

JOKES, GAGS, AND TEASERS

I betcha I can make three squares with three matches. If I'm wrong, will you buy me a drink?

I'm wrong. Now buy me a drink.

I'll give you a dime for every quarter that you balance on edge. If he succeeds in balancing the quarter on its edge, reach for same and give him a dime for it. Remind him that you said you would give a dime for the quarter.

When you spelled weather "w-h-e-t-h-e-r," the teacher said, "That's about the worst spell of weather we've had this year."

Doctor's wife: "John, why did you cut out the back part of the book I bought you?"

Doctor: "Oh, dear, I thought it was marked 'appendix' and I removed it."

I am something that every living person has seen, but no one will ever see me again. What am I?

Yesterday.

How many books can a student put in an empty bag?

    One; after that, the bag isn't empty.

What musical instrument has had an honorary degree conferred upon it?

    Fiddle D.D.

What did old King Neptune say when the seas dried up?

    "I haven't an ocean" (a notion).

What is the longest sentence in the world?

    "Go to prison for life."

If your left arm was cut off, would your right arm be left?

What should you always do with your eyes?

    Dot them.

What is the worth of a woman?

    W (double you) O man.

Why is a crossword like a quarrel?

    Because one word leads to another.

JOKES, GAGS, AND TEASERS

How many peas in a pint?

> One p.

What is the difference between a glass of H^{20} and a glass of whiskey?

> A dollar.

Why is twice ten like twice eleven?

> Twice ten is twenty and twice eleven is twenty too (twenty-two).

How do you spell "blind pig"?

> B-l-n-d p-g. You have to spell it that way because a blind pig has no eyes.

"Mom told me, ma'am," said the teacher's pet, "that you were stuck up." Then he said, "How much did they get?"

Boy: "Ouch, this liniment makes my arm smart."
Teacher: "Why don't you put some on your head?"

Which will burn longer—a wax or a tallow candle?

> Neither. They will both burn shorter.

Two children both boys, were born of the same mother at the same time, yet they were not twins. How is this possible?

They were triplets.

Transform the word *hole* into a building with two pencil lines ("T").

Hole—*hotel*.

Draw a large capital D. Inside it, draw an apple. If this picture was on an envelope, to what city would you sent it?

In *D* an apple is ... Indianapolis.

Ask someone to say "Ohwa tagoo siam" as fast as he can. After three or four times, it will sound like, "Oh, what a goose I am."

Repeat to someone the sentence: "Silly Sally saw Sam." Now ask how many *S*s are in it; when he tells you four, ask him again, with a pained expression in your eyes, whether it has any *S*s at all.

He'll admit he's an "ass."

Betcha you can't tell me why they call language the mother tongue.

> Because father never gets a chance to use it.

A teacher, taking over a new class, asked a little boy his name. "Jule," he replied. "Not Jule," she said. "You shouldn't use contractions. Your name is Julius." Turning to the next boy, she asked: "And what is your name?" "Billious," he replied.

Arthur: "Where was Solomon's temple?"
Martha: "Beats me. Where?"
Arthur: "On the side of his head."

How did a man get out of a locked and barred house in which the only piece of furniture was a table?

> He rubbed his hands until they were sore. Then he sawed the table in half. Two halves made a whole. He hollered through the hole until he was hoarse; then he jumped on the horse and rode away.

When is a piece of wood like a queen?

> When it is made into a ruler.

A penny-pinching penguin, asked by his son to explain the difference between valor and discretion, replied, "*Valor*, my boy, is dining in a high-class restaurant and not tipping the waiter. *Discretion* is eating at another place next time!"

How did Miss Talkative go crazy?

> She tried to have the last word with an echo.

Why is a woman, when blindfolded, like an ignorant schoolteacher?

> Because her pupils are kept in the dark.

When a librarian goes fishing, what does she use for bait?

> Bookworms.

Tommy Tucker took two strings and tied two turtles to two tall trees. How many *T*s are there in that?

> To be perfectly frank, there are only two *T*s in "that."

What three authors do you call out when you burn yourself?

> Dickens Howitt Burns

How can it be proved that a horse has six legs?

    He has fore (four) legs in front and two behind.

What question can never be answered by "yes"?

    Are you asleep?

What does the letter *B* do for boys as they grow older?

    It makes older boys bolder.

Spell donkey in three letters.

    Y-o-u.

If a machine with three wheels is a *tri*cycle and one with two wheels is a bicycle, why isn't one with one wheel an icicle and one with five wheels a V-hicle?

To what question must you positively answer "yes"?

    What does y-e-s spell?

What is the last thing a person takes off before going to bed?

    His *feet* off the floor.

2
Word Play

I betcha I can write faster than you.

> Write "faster than you" on a piece of paper.

I betcha you can't put four feet against the wall.

> Place the feet of a chair against the wall.

There were six teacups on a shelf. One fell down. How many were left?

> Fifty-nine. (If they say five cups were left, you said sixty cups.)

I betcha I can make you talk Indian.

> *How?* That's right.

I betcha I can guess your weight as close as you can.

> Ask him what he guesses his weight is. Suppose he says 130 pounds. Then you say: "Well, I guess it to be 130 pounds," which is as close as he is.

Pick up a book and hand it to a friend, telling him to turn to any page and read a few lines from any passage he chooses. You say: "I betcha I can tell you what goes next without looking into the book; pick any part you want; you can start in the middle of a paragraph and I'll tell you what goes next."

> He reads two or three lines and stops, waiting for you to say what goes next, and that's exactly what you do. You say, clearly enunciating, "What goes next," which is just what you promised to say.

I betcha you can't say light without heat.

> Most people will keep on saying "light without heat" until they realize that all you want them to say is "light" without saying "heat."

WORD PLAY

Ask someone to spell three words in the English language. The first word to be spelled is *receive*. The second word is *believe*. After these are spelled correctly, you laughingly say, "Wrong," saying nothing more but repeating it several times. After the victim insists that he is right, suggest a fresh start, and after *believe* you again say, "Wrong." Eventually, he'll discover that "wrong" was the last of the three words.

I betcha you can't spell New York backward. Or can you spell it backward?

> After they've tried, you say *it* is t-i (backward).

How do you pronounce the capital of Kentucky—Louisville or Loowiville?

> The capital is Frankfort.

How do you pronounce "to," "two," "too"?

What is the second day of the week?

> Tuesday? No, the second day of the week is Monday.

How do you pronounce j-o-k-e? C-o-k-e? P-o-k-e? What is the white of an egg called?

    Y-o-l-k? No, the white of an egg is the albumen.

How do you pronounce So-met-i-mes?
    Sometimes.

How do you pronounce bac-kac-he?
    Backache.

How do you pronounce cho-pho-use?
    Chophouse.

How do you pronounce Mac-Cor-mack? Mac-In-tyre? Mac-hin-ery?
    MacCormack; MacIntyre; machinery

How do you spell Constantinople?

    When the person reaches C-o-n-s-t-a-n-t-i, call out, "No." Each time he comes to C-o-n-s-t-a-n-t-i, call out, "No." Unless he knows the trick, the person will begin the spelling again and again.

I betcha you can't count the alphabet backward as fast as I can.

>Turn your back to the opponent and say the alphabet forward: A, B, C, etc.

Jumping over the haystack—Chairs and other furniture are piled up in the center of the room to a considerable height. The leader says to the victim: "Do you see these chairs arranged in a pile? Take off your shoes and jump over them." The victim surveys the pile and insists that it cannot be done. The catch is that the player is supposed to jump over his shoes.

Hold up four items—a dime, a key, a penny, and a cigarette lighter. Betcha don't know which is lighter.

>The lighter.

Betcha you don't know when up means down.

>When a house burns up, it burns down.

I betcha I can make a sentence out of nine zeros.

>Draw five verticle lines to get this effect: 0000 000 00. "Good God Go."

BIG BLUE BAMBOOZLE

Try this on a friend, but make him answer quickly. Ask him to tell you the opposite of "not in." He's almost sure to say "out." But the opposite of "not in" is "*in.*"

Bite an inch off the pencil. A pencil is held about an inch from the face, making a bite—of course, the person does not bite the pencil but "an inch off the pencil."

Can you form *one word* from the letters in "new room"?

> You couldn't, even after being told "from ... *one word.*"

A Dangerous Position—The player is required to sit upon the fire. This is done by writing the words *the fire* on a slip of paper and then sitting on it.

I betcha I can write a longer word than you can, no matter how long a word you write.

> Write: "A longer word than you can."

WORD PLAY

Super Mindreading—Give a person a piece of paper and tell him to write something. You also write something that he can't see. Write the word *no*. Ask him if he knows what you wrote. He'll say, "No." You say, "That's right."

You've read his mind.

I betcha you can't say "fish" with your mouth closed.

Say, "Fish with your mouth closed."

Boy: Betcha I can make you say "purple."
Girl: Bet you can't.
Boy: What color are your eyes?
Girl: Blue.
Boy: What is the color of your blouse?
Girl: Green.
Boy: I told you I could make you say "green."
Girl: You said purple, not green.
Boy: You just said it.

Betcha you can't immediately tell me one hundred words that *don't* contain the letters A,B,C,J,K,M,P,Q,X,Y,Z.

Count from one to one hundred.

BIG BLUE BAMBOOZLE

Betcha can't tell me where to find the following sites: Island of Reil, McBurney's Point, and the Tunnel of Corti.

They're all parts of the human body!

3

Stunts—Physical and Psychological

To a pretty girl: I betcha a dollar I can kiss you without touching you.

> It cannot be done. But we take it you're man enough to pay a dollar for a kiss. It should be worth it. (In order to lose the bet, ask her to close her eyes, and then kiss her.)

I betcha you can't button up your coat, jacket, or shirt in ten seconds.

> I watched you. You buttoned it down.

I betcha I have more hair on my head than you have.

> Extract a hair from his head and say: "Now you have one less hair than before."

I betcha I can keep you from walking forward without holding you or tying you up.
> Put him against the wall, facing it.

I betcha I can tear an ordinary paper napkin twisted into a rope.
> Moisten your thumb, which will soften the napkin. The moist tissue will tear easily.

I betcha two small boys can lift you up by the elbows if your hands are pointing up.
> Two strong men will not be able to lift the same person if he relaxes his muscles and slouches.

I betcha I can make you motion with your hands within five minutes.
> Distract the player by asking questions that require yes-or-no answers. Then, when he has apparently forgotten about the bet, ask:
> 1. What is a spiral staircase?
> 2. What is a Van Dyke beard?

I betcha that I can put my foot on a chair before you do. Give the player a head start.
> He will put his shoe on a chair. You take off your shoe and put your *foot* on the chair.

STUNTS

Borrow a finger ring and place it over a pencil. Have someone hold both ends of the pencil to keep the ring from slipping off. "I betcha I can take the ring off the pencil without removing your hands."

Lift the ring and hold so that it does not touch the pencil, even though the pencil is still running through the ring.

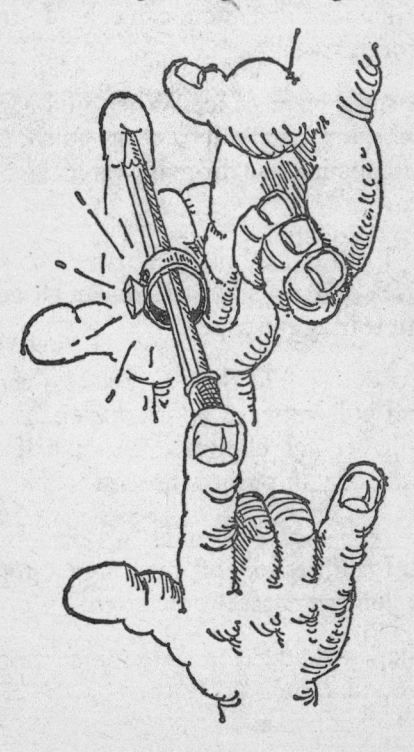

Betcha you will not be able to jump over this pencil if I place it three inches off the ground.

> Place the pencil against the wall so he will not be able to jump over it.

Betcha I can hold something in my hand for three minutes that you can't hold in your hand for thirty seconds.

> A small piece of ice. When you hand the cube, or what's left of it, it should be just about a few drops of water.

Betcha I can cut a hole in a paper the size of a quarter and place a half dollar through it without tearing the paper.

> To do so, fold the paper across the hole and pull outward on the paper. The hole will become elongated and a half dollar can easily be pushed through.

Betcha I can tie four of your fingers together so that you can not leave the room.

> Tie his thumb and index finger together around a door knob, then do the same to his other hand.

STUNTS

Betcha that two people can stand on a newspaper and yet will not be able to touch each other.

> Place a newspaper on the floor under a door and have each member stand on the paper but on opposite sides of the door.

Bet the cook of the house that if you give all the ingredients to bake a cake, he cannot do it.

> One of the ingredients you give is eggs (which you have *hard-boiled* previously).

Bet that I can light a match under running water.

> Sit under the sink while the water's running and light the match.

Place any two objects in your hand and bet that no one can tell you exactly how many items you hold.

> Regardless of what the answer is, say: "Nope." After a while, say: "There are three articles. If I'm wrong, will you give me a quarter? . . . Okay, I'm wrong, give me the quarter."

BIG BLUE BAMBOOZLE

Betcha I can make you close your eyes and then open them again.

> "Close your eyes . . . no, no, no—not *that* way. . . ." When he opens his eyes to see *which* way, he loses the bet.

Bet the wise guy that he can't place his head against the wall, standing three feet away from it, then regain his original straight position without first moving his hands or feet.

> Try this. You'll like it.

Bet a person that he can't blow out a candle if he is blindfolded and turned around three times.

> Blindfold and turn him. Then *you* blow out the candle. He not only loses, but watch him blow his head off.

Tell a player that he may choose any partner. Then tell him that they will both be blindfolded, and bet him that as they walk towards each other from opposite sides of the room, they will not be able to shake hands with each other.

> Take the blindfold off one. Wink—and watch the other poor soul take a trip for himself.

STUNTS

Two players are blindfolded and are to feed each other dry cereal. Bet that both bowls will not be emptied in three minutes of feeding each other.

> Remove the blindfold from one player and let him in on the gag.

Place a drop of water on the edge of a table and bet that if a person will concentrate and look very closely at the drop of water, he will see dancing spots and little stars. (Only bet a penny.)

> When he places his eyes near the drop of water, *slam* your hand down on the table, splashing the water into his eyes. Did you see the stars?

Betcha I can take a picture of you that will make you smile.

> With a camera in hand and with blackened fingers (which the victim doesn't see), adjust his face—turn him sideways, forward, any way—as you continually blacken his face. Then snap his picture (with or without film), and hand him a mirror.

BIG BLUE BAMBOOZLE

Betcha you will have to admit that this one is a good trick. "Does anyone have a cigar?"

> They will offer you a cigar, obviously thinking it's for a trick. This you will light and puff on, and show them a trick . . . any trick. (Thank the donor for the cigar.)

I betcha you can't remove your jacket alone.

> As he starts to remove his jacket, you remove yours also. He therefore is not removing it alone.

Betcha I can tear a telephone directory in half.

> Use an old address book that you no longer need, and tear it in half.

"Oh, you mean a regular telephone directory? Okay, you have a bet."

> Bend the phonebook sideways and tear the pages with a quick pull as you hold the pages on an angle. This permits, in effect, the tearing of one page at a time.

Betcha I can draw a circle around you that you won't get out of.

> With chalk, draw a circle around his waist.

STUNTS

Bet I can make you put your arms up. . . .
Okay, then I bet I can make you put your hands down.

> This makes him put his hands up. You win that bet. Sooner or later he'll put his hands down. You win again.

Betcha that with a three-inch piece of string I can tie you so you can't escape.

> Have the victim lie on his stomach and bend his knees so that his feet go as far back as possible. Then bring his hands back to encircle his ankles. Then tie his thumbs together.

I betcha my pencil can write several different colors. Ask the players to call out the different colors and don't let them see your writing until the end.

> All you do when they call out the colors is to write out the words: "yellow," "red," etc.

I betcha you can't intertwine your fingers.

> Place your fingers over his and he will be at your mercy.

I betcha I can have three pieces of paper on the back of my hand and only blow off the two that you select.

> Place a finger on the selected piece and blow the other two pieces off.

I betcha you can't get up alone.

> Stand up simultaneously with your friend.

Have your friend stand up or sit up on a bar stool. Say to him: "I betcha I can make you get off the stool."

> You leave him and eventually he will get off and gradually catch on to the idea.

I betcha I can make a match burn twice.

> Light a match. Blow it out. Gently touch your victim with it. It will burn him.

STUNTS

Problem: You have placed a dollar bill on the floor and stood a Dixie cup on one end of it. You have had a friend stand with his toes at the other end of the bill. Yet he can't jump over the cup.

Why? Simple! The end of the dollar bill with the cup on it is against the wall.

BIG BLUE BAMBOOZLE

Have a strong individual hold a common broomstick horizontally in front of him. Have him place his hands about three feet apart. Stand in front of him on one foot. Place the tip of your thumb against the broomstick and challenge him to unbalance you.

> Use a slight upward pressure with your thumb. Push the broomstick sufficiently out of the horizontal position so that the holder will require more strength than he possesses to counteract the upward movement. All his efforts will be expended trying to hold the broomstick down instead of pushing it against you.

Draw a six-inch circle on the floor, and place a coin in the center of the circle. Have three players grip the broomstick near the upper end, and tell them to hold the broomstick a foot above the coin. Bet them that with only one finger you can prevent them from pushing the broomstick down so that it lands on the coin.

> Place any finger about three inches from the bottom of the broomstick. If you apply a little pressure, you will prevent the stick from coming down vertically.

STUNTS

Take two corks of the same size and of equal diameter at top and bottom. Stand the corks ends up on a table, side by side, touching each other. Ask if anyone present can lift the two corks together between the ends of the index and second fingers of one hand.

> Unless you hold your fingers in a particular manner, the corks will roll away every time the fingers try to grasp them. (The secret is to bend the fingers slightly at both the first and second joints. With the fingers bent in this fashion, the corks can readily be picked up between the very tips of the fingers.)

Betcha I can make you blink without touching you.

> Slap your hands smartly before his face.

Betcha I can make you blink by saying only one word.

> Blow in his eyes as you say, "What."

Place a piece of paper in a penciled circle and bet that you can remove the paper with just a whisper.

> Blow on the paper as you pronounce "whisper."

Betcha I can prevent you from walking forward, using only one finger.

> Place your finger above his lip, under his nose. This is a pressure point and he will not be able to come forward.

Bet someone that you can place him in a position that he will be unable to lift his left foot from the floor, although it is free.

> Stand him against the wall with his right cheek touching it and his right foot also touching the wall. Now tell him to try and lift his left foot.

Stunts

Can you rub the crown of your head with a circular motion of your left hand and at the same time pat your stomach with your right hand? Have you perfect control of the motions of both hands?

Can you draw a clockwise circle while moving your right foot counterclockwise? (Use your left foot if left-handed.)

STUNTS

Cross or interlock two fingers, middle and index. Touch your nose with the tips of the fingers and you will feel two noses.

Clasp your fingers (interlock) and extend your index fingers together and open them. They will come together by themselves.

Have a friend cross his hands and then clasp fingers tightly; then ask him to reverse the tightly clasped hands, holding them near the chin. Now bet him that he will always move the finger opposite that to which you will point. This is due to the intertwining of the nerves, and as long as you don't touch the finger you want moved, but just point to it, he will always move the finger opposite it. At the moment that he moves the finger, it feels as if he is really moving the finger designated. But, to his surprise, the other finger rises. Should you, however, touch the finger, the nerves seem to identify themselves and act in accordance.

This is one of those too-too easy stunts that turn out otherwise. Balance a cork on the neck of a bottle. Then, from about ten feet away, walk swiftly forward toward the bottle, one arm extended with thumb and middle finger in "snapping position"—and without hesitation snap the cork from the bottle. If you can do it in three tries, you're good. Once you're on the beam, you can do it every time.

STUNTS

Touch the tips of two pencils held at arm's length. Easy, isn't it? Now try it with one eye closed. The result may surprise you. To make the test purely one of vision, drop your arms out of position between each attempt.

Close one eye and try to touch the tips of your index fingers together by holding the arms apart, aiming the fingers at each other, and drawing them together.

Circle your right foot to the left and your right hand to the right at the same time. You will find it very difficult.

Ask a friend to start moving his right foot around in a circle going clockwise. When he gets started, ask him to keep it up but at the same to make a figure 6 with his right hand. On no account is he to change the motion of his right foot.

At a party, line up a few people, each of whom had previously measured four lengths, according to each individual foot, from a cork lying on the floor.
Now, the bet is that not one of them can, with one foot, kick over the cork and recover his original position (both feet together) without the foot that does the kicking touching the floor till it has returned to its

mate. They will find it impossible to maintain their equilibrium.

Two players at a time can have fun with this one. The first puts his finger on his ear and says: "This is my eyebrow—one, two, three, four, five, six, seven, eight, nine, ten!"

Before he reaches the count of ten, the other player must put his finger on his *eyebrow* and say: "This is my *ear*." (You'll be surprised how easy it is to get mixed up in this game.)

If the second player makes a mistake, the first has a chance to go again. This time, he may point to his hair and say: "This is my teeth—one, two, three," and so on. The first player keeps on having a turn until the second one answers without making a mistake.

Bet someone that he can't make his fists twirl in opposite directions—one fist twirling away from the body, while the other fist twirls toward the body.

It is noteworthy of our attention how the so-called cooperation between muscle and brain works here to such an extent that the latter at times cannot control the messages it transmits to the former. Just try it sometimes for the result.

STUNTS

Other Stunts

Have a subject sit in a chair, with his head tilted back. By placing your index finger against his forehead and applying pressure, subject will be unable to rise.

You can bet some unusually "tough egg" that if he held an ordinary egg (hard-boiled) between the palms of his hands in such a way that both ends of the egg rested securely against the centers of his palms, he couldn't break it no matter what amount of pressure he applied. You can even let him place his hands between his knees (as long as he holds it properly, because a slight tilt of the egg from the central line will immediately smash it).

Have someone bend over and place his fingers beneath his toes and then bet him that in this position he can jump backward farther than he can forward. Fear not, you will be successful.

STUNTS

We often wonder whether it is possible to attend to two mental operations at the same time. By trying this experiment, you will be able to answer the question.

Recite the alphabet aloud and write it backward at the same time. Or—count aloud by sevens (seven, fourteen, twenty-one, etc.) as fast as you can while writing the letters of the alphabet at the same time.

A good bet that will always work is to bet that one of the tall glasses they serve beer in is larger around the diameter at the top than it is tall. It looks impossible, but measure with a piece of string and you will win. This works with all tall glasses.

Place three glasses next to one another. The first two are filled with water and the last is empty.

Bet anyone that you can place the empty glass between the two filled glasses by moving only one glass, while he cannot.

Answer: Pour water from the middle glass into the empty glass. The center glass will then be empty, and you will win.

This is a highly provocative proceeding and will cause a lot of comment. You wager anybody that if he or she should raise one arm for about two minutes while you are not in the room, you will be able to tell, immediately upon return, which hand was raised. And there is no need for an accomplice.

When you return to the room, examine both hands; note which hand is redder than the other, and you will know that the pale hand is the one that was held aloft.

(It's all very simple. As the hand is raised, the blood leaves it and flows down into the body. The other hand is "flooded" by contrast and you will have no difficulty distinguishing between the two.)

It is possible to witness the beating of the pulse. Place a match upright on the point of a thumbtack. Stand the head of the tack on the wrist at the place where the pulse can be felt. The head of the match will bow with each pulse beat. It is oddly interesting!

STUNTS

If you place the ends of two pencils on the back of someone's neck, he will not be able to tell if there are one or two pencils, because the nerve endings in that part of the body are far apart.

Ask someone to stand with his back against the wall and make sure that his heels touch the wall. Put a quarter in front of him and challenge him to pick it up without bending his knees or removing his heels from their position. It is almost impossible to pick up the coin from this position.

Take a glass of water and hold it at arm's length. Challenge someone to hold your hand and prevent your drinking the water. Let him take a strong grip on your arm and tell him that you will bring the glass to your lips and drink it. After he has applied a strong grip, take the glass with your *free* hand and drink from it.

BIG BLUE BAMBOOZLE

Place a strip of thin board, or a long, wide, flat ruler, on the edge of a table so that it just balances itself, and spread over it an ordinary newspaper.

You may now hit it quite hard with your doubled fist, or with a stick, and it will remain as firmly in its place as if it were glued to the table. You are more likely to break the stick which you strike with than to displace the strip of wood or paper.

Set a stool on the floor about nine or ten inches from the wall. Clasp it firmly by its two edges (sides) and rest your head against the wall. Now lift the stool and try, without moving your feet, to recover an upright position.

Place a stool on the floor against the wall. Have somebody stand away from the wall with his feet spread apart twice the width of the stool. Tell him to stoop down and seize the stool by the top in both hands and to place the top of his head against the wall so that his back is almost horizontal.

Now bet him that he can't lift the stool from the ground alone. It is advisable to have a soft carpet on the floor. His failure is due to a curious effect of the displacement of his center of gravity, which makes it almost impossible to raise himself to the perpendicular position without dropping the stool to the ground.

Suspend a ring by a string on a level with the eyes, with the plane of the ring toward the person. Tie a small stick crosswise on the end of another about a yard long. Hold the long stick, shut one eye, and try to thread the ring with the crossed stick. Success will scarcely be attained, but if both eyes are used the ring can be threaded at the first attempt.

This trick may be varied by using only a crooked stick instead of two sticks tied crosswise.

Chinese Get Up—Hold one arm and lie on the floor. Get up without using hands or elbows.

Knee Balance—Kneel on both knees and fold arms behind the back. Place a handkerchief in wigwam fashion on the floor about eighteen inches in front. Bend over and pick up the handkerchief with the lips without losing balance. The handkerchief must be placed the right distance in front, depending on the size of the individual—too close and it is no stunt at all; too far and it cannot be done.

STUNTS

Hawk Dive—Place a handkerchief on the floor and kneel on the right knee about six inches from the handkerchief. Raise the left leg behind and grasp it with the left hand, using the right hand for balance. Bend down and pick up the handkerchief with the mouth. No part of the body but the right leg may touch the floor.

Head Pivot—Draw a line two feet from the wall. Stand with toes against this line, facing the wall. Place the head against the wall, and fold the arms behind back. Using the head as a pivot, circle the body around and back to the original position without crossing the line or removing the head from the wall.

Chair Bend—Place a handkerchief on the floor eighteen inches in front of a straight-back chair. Sit on the chair facing backward. Fold the arms and clasp the legs around the legs of the chair. Bend over backward, pick up the handkerchief with the mouth, and come up to sitting position again. The chair should be steadied by someone. Careful, this is a back-breaker!

BIG BLUE BAMBOOZLE

Dime On a Nose—Ask the player to lie flat on his back on the floor. Place a dime on his nose so that it rests perfectly horizontal. Tell him to wiggle his nose and put the dime off. He cannot do it.

Bear Dance—Squat on one heel. Extend the other foot forward. With the back straight and arms extended forward for balance, rapidly shift the position of the feet.

Stand on either foot with opposite leg extended forward off floor. Squat on heel of leg on floor without touching free leg or hands to floor or losing the balance. Return to standing position, keeping the balance.

Fold arms on chest, sit down cross-legged, and get up without unfolding arms or losing balance.

4

Tongue Twisters—
To Be Read Only
When Sober

These tongue twisters can be used at parties and similar occasions. One leader or master of ceremonies may ask for several members to recite a series of these tongue twisters; and the rest of the party members or a committee will decide which person is the winner.

They may also be used as a game in itself or as a spare in a game program.

What a shame such shapely sashes show such shabby stilted stitches.

A skunk sat on a stump. The skunk thunk the stump stunk, but the stump thunk the skunk stunk.

Good blood, bad blood. (Five times.)

Smith's fish-sauce shop seldom sells shellfish.

BIG BLUE BAMBOOZLE

Peter Piper picked a peck of pickled peppers; a peck of pickled peppers did Peter Piper pick.

Five Fanny Farmers feeding feathered fowls.

Sarah sits by six sick city slickers.

Three thumping thrush thoroughly thwarting thirty thrashers.

Eve eating eagerly elegant Easter eggs.

Fresh flesh of fresh fried fish.

Four fat friars fanning flickering flames.

Sister Susie's swiftly sewing sixty shirts in sixty seconds.

Two tiny timid toads trotting in Tarrytown.

Ten tiny titmice tipping ten tall tamarack trees.

Sarah in a shawl shoveled soft snow softly.

Six thick thistle sticks stick thistles.

A thistle sifter has a sieve of sifted thistles and a sieve of unsifted thistles.

Quiz kids quiz quizzically.

Did David Daldrom dream he drove a dragon? Draw the wagon David Daldrom dreamt he drove.

Three tinkering tailors totally tired.

TONGUE TWISTERS

Theophilus Thistle thrust three thousand thistles through his thick thumb.

Bitter bickering bricklayers bickering bitterly.

Seven social showmen socially showing soaps.

The block bootblack blacks boots black.

Six slipper stitchers slyly stitching slippers.

Rubber baby buggy bumper. (Five times.)

Shy Sunshine Sue shuns sunshine.

A growing glowing glow bug gleams green.

She sheds unshedded shawls.

The sea seetheth and it sufficeth us.

Twisting two twigs on two twisted tree trunks.

Bristling bustles in Brussels.

She says she shaves a cedar shingle thin.

A sinning skin shuns sunshine.

Abdominal abominable. (Five times.)

Six shrews shoved Sue's sheep.

Should Shoeshine Sam shrewdly sell slippery shrimps?

The blue bluebird blinks.

Sweater Sam sweats while swatting sweaters.

Amiable Annabelle emanates animation.

Blue blood, black blood.

The whistling whistler wets his whistle.

Blackbeard brought back black bricabrac.

Chief Sheep cheapens sheep.

Which wristwatch will rich Willie wish to wear?

School coal scuttles.

A box of biscuits, a box of mixed biscuits, a biscuit mixer.

Slick super sleuth.

Wicked witches which switch.

Massaging messenger messages masseurs.

Special specifics specify species.

The break brought the bike back.

Peeking Piper pecks proudly.

Blue big blister bleeding badly.

Pornographic phenomenal phonograph.

Phone faunting fans frequently.

Flaunt fawning fancies.

Skim Sanders slapped silly Sue.

Cool clean canned clams.

TONGUE TWISTERS

Brats break basting bats.

Sleepy city slops slapping surreptitiously.

Glad Gladys grabbed glibly.

Mix, Miss Mix. (Five times.)

Sister Susie still stitches sugar sacks slowly.

Thoughtful Terry Thatcher taught thoughtful thespians.

One smart fellow he felt smart; two smart fellows they felt smart; three smart fellows they all felt smart.

Capitalists capitulate connectively.

Prescriptive scripting subscribes prescription.

Proportions perpetuating peripatetically.

Cynical cycles circle incessantly.

Pitcher patches panting pitchers.

Shaping slim ships shipshape.

Fighting fire-fighters fight frantically.

Round and round the rugged rocks the rugged wheel ran.

She's so selfish she should sell shellfish, but shellfish shells seldom sell.

BIG BLUE BAMBOOZLE

Betty Blue blows big black bubbles.

Two toads totally tired tried to trot to Tetbutty.

Vera bastes vests and waists.

A crop of poppies in a copper coffeepot.

Seven slick slimy snakes sliding slowly southward.

Tillie's twin sweater set.

Poor find for poor.

Across crossings cross cautiously.

The soldier's shoulder strap slipped from the soldier's shoulder.

Needling nine needles needlessly.

Knotting nine knots neatly.

Baking broken bricks briskly.

Peter parts prickly pears.

Chatting chits cite chidingly.

Prince prances prettily.

Daring daredevils dive daily.

Gaunt giants gesticulate garishly.

Lawyer slays slavish slayer.

Mrs., mistress, master, mister.

Praying priests pray patiently.

Betty Battor bought a bit of bitter butter, but she said, "This butter is bitter, but a bit of better butter will make my batter better." So Betty Battor bought a bit of better butter and made her batter better.

More Tongue Twisters

Betcha you can't repeat these tongue twisters—and some you can't even read without stepping on your tongue.

Does your shirt shop stock short sox with spots?

Tongue twisters twist tongues twisted trying to untangle twisted tangles. My tang's tungled now.

"Go my son and shut the shutter."
This I head a mother utter.
"Shutter's shut," the boy did mutter,
"I can't shut 'er any shutter."

I saw Esaw kissing Kate,
Fact is, we all three saw.
I saw Esaw, he saw me,
and she saw I saw Esaw.

Each sixth chick sat on a stick.

Of all the saws I ever saw, I never saw a saw saw like that saw saws.

Six slim slick slender saplings.

Round and round the rugged rock the ragged rascal ran.

Now here are some that you might try repeating three times:

The sun shines on the shop signs.

Truly rural.

Sixty-six sick chicks.

Lemon liniment.

Tie twine to the tree twigs.

Strange strategic statistics.

> A tooter who tooted the flute
> Tried to tutor two tooters to boot;
> Said the two to the tutor,
> "Is it harder to toot
> Than to tutor two tooters to toot?"

Esaw Wood sawed wood. Esaw Wood would saw wood. Oh, the wood Wood would saw. One day Esaw Wood saw a saw saw wood as no other wood saw would saw wood. In fact, of all the wood saws Wood ever saw wood,

TONGUE TWISTERS

Wood never saw a wood saw that would saw wood as the wood saw Wood Saw saw wood, and I never saw a wood saw that would saw as the wood saw Wood saw would until I saw Esaw Wood saw wood with the wood saw that Wood saw saw wood.

He sighed, she sighed, they both sighed, side by side, down beside the riverside.

How much dew could a dewdrop drop if a dewdrop could drop dew?

A big black bug bit a big black bear on the end of his big black nose.

Bill had a billboard. Bill also had a board bill. The board bill bored Bill, so Bill sold the billboard to pay his board bill. So after Bill sold his billboard to pay his board bill, the board bill no longer bored Bill.

If a twists a twister and a twist that twists the twister untwists the twister, what becomes of the twist that untwists the twister?

Sam Slick sawed six slim slippery slender sticks.

How much wood would a woodchuck chuck if a woodchuck could chuck wood.

Betcha can't say three times rapidly:

> Black bug's blood.
> The sixth sick sheik's sixth sheep's sick.

Given *three* tries, bet you can't repeat this one:

> Whiskey makes you well when you're sick.
>
> Whiskey when you're well makes you sick.

5

Wagers with Coins and Bills and Other Money Betchas

I betcha you cannot tell what money I hold in my hand. Odds or even?

> You hold a dime, a nickel, and five pennies. If the guesser says "odd," you count ten cents for the dime, five cents for the nickel, and five pennies, and say, "Twenty cents, that's even." If the guesser says "even," you count the coins singly, and say "seven coins, that's odd."

I betcha a dollar that if you give me two dollars, I'll give you back four dollars.

> After he gives you the two dollars, say "I can't do it after all." Then give him back one of his two dollars. After all, you lost the bet, but you keep the other dollar.

I betcha you can't pick up a penny lying near the edge of a table without touching the coin.

> Place your half-opened hand a short distance in back of the coin. Blow sharply upon the table several inches in front of the coin, and the blast of air will lift it up into your hand. Do not blow down upon the coin; blow along the surface of the table.

I betcha I can make the pennies I'm holding in each hand exchange positions without opening my hands.

> Cross your arms so that the left hand is on the right and the right hand is on the left.

I betcha I can transfer the coin I'm holding in my right hand to my left hand without bringing my hands together.

> Step over to a table and drop the coin on the table and then, turning halfway around, pick it up with the other hand.

WAGERS AND MONEY BETCHAS

I betcha I can toss off any one of the three pennies which I placed on the back of my hand without losing the other two coins.

> Have your victim select the coin that you are to toss off. The catch is that you put two fingers on the rejected coins. It is now an easy matter to toss off the selected penny.

I betcha I can make the eagle on a fifty-cent piece wet itself if I squeeze his belly.

> Conceal a small ball of wet tissue paper between the first two fingers of the right hand. The eagle will wet simply by squeezing together the fingers holding the wet paper.

I betcha I can push a half dollar through a hole in a cardboard the width of a pencil.

> Push a pencil through a hole and then proceed to push the coin.

BIG BLUE BAMBOOZLE

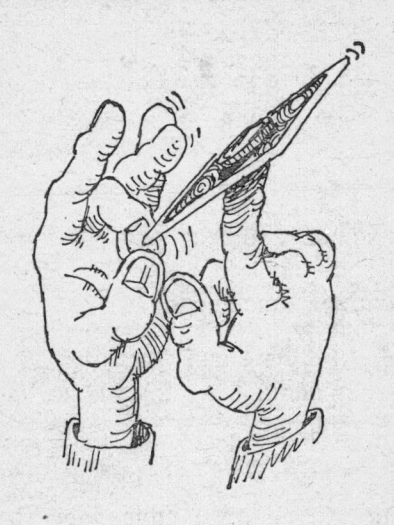

Place a playing card on your finger and place a coin on the card. Without holding either the coin or the card, bet you can remove the card from your finger without the coin.

> With your other hand, snap the card off your finger as you would shoot a marble. If you snap the card straight off quickly, the coin will not drop to the floor.

Hold your elbow out parallel with the floor and pile five nickels on your elbow. Bet you can catch all five nickels with the same hand without dropping any nickels.

> It's simply a matter of practice. A slow and easy motion does the trick. Don't try to do it fast or be overanxious.

Place a dime, a nickle, and a penny on a table. Bet you can remove the nickel from the center without touching it.

> Take the dime and place it to the right of the penny; The nickel is no longer in the center.

Place three coins on a table. Pick them up one at a time, saying as you do it, "One, two, three." Lay them on the table, saying "Four, five, six." Pick up two, saying, "Seven, eight," and, pointing to the remaining one, say, "An extra one." Put down the two in your hand and say, "Nine, ten." Challenge a friend to do the same thing. When he accepts the challenge, pick up the coins and place them in his hand. Everyone counts the coins as they put them down. If asked to do it again, refuse—cautioning him about the extra one.

WAGERS AND MONEY BETCHAS

What U.S. coin will double in value if you take away its half?

> A half dollar. If you take away ½ it becomes 1.

Take seven coins; place four vertically one after the other and next to the top coin place two horizontally. Betcha can't make two rows of four coins by moving one coin.

> Take the last coin on the vertical row and put it on top of the first coin of that row.

I betcha I have between eighteen and nineteen hundred dollars and yet have only a hundred.

> Isn't one hundred the difference between eighteen and nineteen hundred dollars?

Betcha I can guess closer to the date on a coin that neither of us has seen, if you give me two guesses to your one.

> He must make the first guess. You then take one year earlier and one year later than the date *he* guesses.

I bet that between my partner and myself we have a hundred thousand dollars.

>   He lives north of the First National Bank and I live south of it.

Bet I can get into the movies if I really want to. How?

>   Pay the two dollars.

Betcha that if you take any coin out of your pocket I'll tell you the date.

>   Tell him the present date. You didn't promise to tell him the date on the coin.

Betcha can't make eleven cents with two American coins, and one of them isn't a dime.

>   Use a penny and a dime. (The penny isn't a dime.)

Betcha I can tell the date on a coin even if you cover it with a piece of paper.

>   Have the coin placed face up on a table and cover with a piece of paper. Run a pencil back and forth across the paper over the coin. The picture and the date will be visible.

WAGERS AND MONEY BETCHAS

Betcha can't tell me which coins are farthest apart.

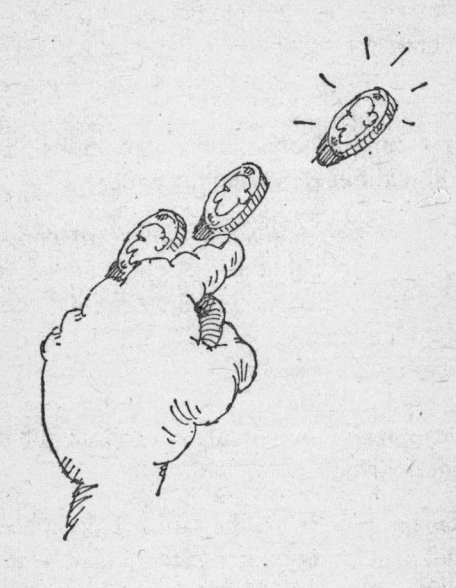

> If he says 2 and 3, point out to him that coin 1 is farther away from 3 than 2 from 3.

Bet they can't toss a coin twenty times and have heads come up five times.

> When they try they will stop when they reach five heads. But the bet was that they would toss it twenty times, *not* stop before twenty.

Bet a penny has a head on one side of the coin and one on the other side.

> There's a head on one side and a *one* (1) cent on the other.

Betcha I can tell the number of coins in a coin roll without removing the paper.

> Rub the package with a piece of carbon paper, then rub the roll back and forth until the impression comes off on a sheet of white paper.

Bet I can make two quarters appear where only one quarter is used.

> Place a quarter on the table. Take a glass and pour some water into it. Then raise the glass slightly and to the right, and you will now see the quarter and its reflection at the same time through the glass of water.

I betcha I have more money in my pocket than you have.

> The opponent has no money in *your* pocket.

WAGERS AND MONEY BETCHAS

After placing a quarter on your forehead, wrinkle your brows, allowing the coin to fall off onto your palm. Now bet that your opponent cannot do the same.

> Secretly wet the coin. Then press it firmly onto his head. Only this time, as you remove your hand, remove also the coin from his head. Watch his facial contortions as he tries to remove the coin, which he feels is still there.

Place a coin on your palm and bet that nobody can brush the coin off your hand with a whisk broom or hair brush.

> This is practically an impossibility unless the coin is manipulated.

Bet that you can put a coin somewhere in the room so that everyone can see it. But—your opponent cannot.

> Place it on his head.

Bet you can't tell me how many heads there are on a quarter.

> *Two*—one on Washington and one on the eagle.

Are there any coins dated 24 B.C.?

> No, How can anything be dated B.C. if C. wasn't known about before he was born?

How many coins are dropped into a box if five jingles are heard each minute for four minutes?

> Twenty-one coins are heard, as the first coin, when the box is empty, will not jingle.

Take eleven pennies and ask someone to remove five coins from the eleven coins; add four and leave nine. Everyone thinks there are ten pennies left.

> From the eleven coins, take five; then add four to those already taken away, and you leave nine in the second heap of those removed.

Place two nickels on a tablecloth. Rest a glass upside down on top of the nickels. Place a dime between the two nickels and under the glass. Bet someone you can get the dime out without touching it or removing the glass.

> Scratch the tablecloth on the outside of the glass. The dime will move toward the scratching finger and you will be able to retrieve it.

WAGERS AND MONEY BETCHAS

Take out two pennies and lay them heads up on a table.

> Bet you can't see the automobiles. (There are two Lincolns.)
> Bet you can't see the snakes! (There are two copperheads.)
> Bet you can't see the pretty girl. (What do you expect for two cents?)

Place a penny on the table and bet that "he" can't find the statue (which is residing within the center columns of the tail side of the coin). You may use a magnifying glass.

Bet I can guess the date on the quarters. I'll give you a dime for every quarter I guess wrong.

> Use *his* quarters, and each time you're wrong, give *him* a dime and keep *his* quarter.

Bet your friend that you can prevent him from having money burn a hole in his pocket.

> As proof, wrap a dollar bill tightly around a quarter or half dollar and touch the glowing end of a cigarette to it. Because of the metal, coin draws off the heat and the bill will not burn.

BIG BLUE BAMBOOZLE

With a pencil, mark one line on one side of a paper match and two lines on the other side. Bet your friend that you will drop the match on the floor, and if it lands with one line up, you will pay him a nickel; two lines up, you will pay him a nickel. If it stands on its edge, he must pay you fifty cents. He gets five chances to win, to your one.

After he wins and totals his nickels and dimes, you casually bend the match and drop it on the floor. It will land on its edge.

WAGERS AND MONEY BETCHAS

Arrange three matches in a triangle on the table; ask him to place a quarter within the triangle. Now—bet him a dime that he will not answer "Three matches" to three questions you ask.

> Will it rain today: (Ans: Three matches.)
> What is this dime made of? (Ans. Three matches.)
> Do you want this quarter or three matches?
>
> (If he says the quarter, give it to him. It was his anyway. But you win the dime. If he says three matches, then keep the quarter and give him a dime because he won the bet.

Betcha don't know which is worth more, a new $5.00 bill or an old one.

> A new $5.00 bill is worth $4.00 more than an old *one dollar bill*.

I betcha you can't find three eyes on a dollar bill.

> On the back of a one-dollar bill, left-hand side, you will find a pyramid. At the top of this pyramid you will find an eye. . . . George Washington has two eyes.

I betcha you can't find a key on a dollar bill.

> On the front of a one-dollar bill, to the right of Washington's picture is a green circle. In the center of this green circle is a key.

I betcha you can't find a scale on a dollar bill.

> On the front of a one-dollar bill, to the right of Washington's picture, is a green circle. In the center of this green circle is a scale.

I betcha you can't find at least seventeen "ones" written and/or numbered on a dollar bill.

> If you include the serial number and look very hard at everything on the dollar, you will discover at least seventeen "ones."

I betcha you can't fold a dollar bill in half eight times. (Can't be done.)

I betcha you can't fix a dollar bill so that it will be impossible to tear.

> Roll a dollar bill from one corner diagonally to the other corner, tightly into a tube.

Stand someone against a wall with his heels together. Place a dollar bill on the floor right in front of him and have him try to pick up the bill while still keeping his heels against the wall, without bending his knees. It is impossible because he will fall forward before he comes near the bill.

I betcha you can't find a mushroom on a dollar bill.

> By folding a one-dollar bill so that Washington's neck rests near the top of his head, you will see a mushroom.

Borrow a dollar bill from someone and put it in a handkerchief with a dollar bill of your own. Offer the contents for a dollar and a half.

> When they buy the bills, they've just paid seventy-five cents for their own dollar.

I betcha you can't break a pencil with a dollar bill.

> Have someone hold a pencil tightly at both ends. Take your dollar bill and fold it in half the long way. Now stick your finger in your dollar and strike the pencil sharply. The pencil will break in two.

Take two glasses and rest a dollar bill on top of them. Bet someone they can't place another glass on top of the bill so that it doesn't topple, and without resting the top glass on either of the two glasses beneath.

Accordion pleat a dollar bill the long way. Fold the bill backward and forward.

I betcha I can put a half dollar in a bottle.

Tear a dollar bill in half and stuff it in the neck of a bottle.

WAGERS AND MONEY BETCHAS

I betcha I can prove it's bad luck to have a two-dollar bill.

Take the two-dollar bill and wrap one of your own one-dollar bills around the two-dollar bill. Ask the owner of the two-dollar bill if he is willing to give two-dollars for both bills, which are wrapped together. When he produces two single dollars, give him the two bills wrapped together and he will have sold his own one-dollar bill for two dollars.

6

Bar Betchas—Using Straws, Glasses, Drinks, and Money

I betcha I can bend a swizzle stick in the middle.

> Place the plastic stirrer in hot water beforehand. While it's hot, it'll be pliable enough to bend.

I betcha I can drink up all the beer and leave enough in a glass for another drink.

> Finish the beer and drop fifteen cents in the glass.

I betcha I can make a head of beer appear on the botton of the glass.

> Put a cardboard on top of the glass and turn the glass upside down.

BIG BLUE BAMBOOZLE

Man at bar: How much is that hard-boiled egg?
Bartender: Thirty-five cents.
Man: How much is a glass of beer?
Bartender: Thirty-five cents.

Man: Give me the beer. I won't take the egg.
Bartender: See here, you haven't paid for the beer.

Man: Of course I haven't. I gave you the egg for it. You said they're both the same price.
Bartender: Yes, but you didn't pay for the egg.

Man: Pay for it! Of course I didn't. Why should I? I didn't take it, did I?

Man at bar: If I leave security equal to what I take away, will you trust me till next week?

Bartender: Certainly.
Man: Well then, sell me two drinks and keep one until I return.

Fill a glass with water and drink it. Holding it upside down, bet that there are still fifty drops in the glass.

> Hold the glass firmly and make a swiping motion at a window or mirror, and more than a hundred drops will appear on it.

Have your victim hold out both his hands, fingers extended, palms down. Then place two full glasses of water on his fingers. Bet the poor lad that he cannot repeat a rhyme without spilling the water.

> This he may do successfully, but will he be in trouble when no one offers to remove the glasses.

Betcha you can't drink from the other side of the cup without getting wet.

> Turn the cup around and drink.

Place a tumbler, with water up to its brim, on a sheet of newspaper, and bet that no one can remove the paper from underneath without spilling a drop of water.

> A quick jerk of the paper *will* spill some water, but if you roll the paper from its folded edge and gradually push the tumbler, it can be accomplished.

Betcha I can overturn a glass of water onto the table without spilling its contents.

> First moisten the rim of the glass containing the water and place a sheet of paper over it. Then invert the glass on a wooden table or other surface and carefully withdraw the paper.

Betcha I can make a glass *whistle*, and you can't.

> Using a cocktail glass, secretly wet your index finger, and slowly—using the fleshy part of your index finger—make a circular motion around the brim of the glass, and the glass will whistle.

BAR BETCHAS

Betcha I can stay under water for a full five minutes.

> Hold a glass of water on your head for five minutes.

You are given a bottle containing a dollar bill. The bottle is sealed with a cork. Bet someone you can remove the bill without breaking the bottle or removing the cork.

> Push the cork in.

Bet a bartender, or a friend, a dollar that you can tell any drink by taste.

> After you've had about three or four drinks and made your guesses, right or wrong, it was worth a dollar to have had all those drinks.

Betcha you can't pick up what I throw down on the floor.

> Spill some water on the floor and challenge your opponent to pick it up.

BIG BLUE BAMBOOZLE

Betcha that you can remove a dollar bill from under an inverted bottle without touching or upsetting the bottle.

Being careful not to touch the bottle with your hands, roll up the bill in such a way that the rolled-up portion gradually shoves the bottle off the bill and onto the table.

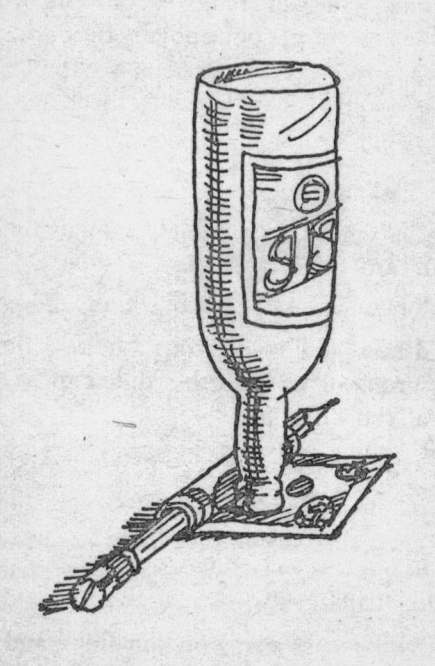

BAR BETCHAS

I betcha I can crawl into that bottle.

> Place a bottle on the floor. Walk back a distance. Then get on your hands and knees and proceed to crawl into the bottle. (Not into—but *in to*.)

Place a strip of heavy paper across the top of a drinking glass. Now bet a member of the group that you can get a coin, which you place upon the paper, into the glass without touching the coin.

> Light the paper with a match. When the paper burns, the coin will fall into the glass.

Betcha I can swallow this drink that you may place under a hat without my touching the hat.

> Go through various antics, then say: "It's gone." When the challenger picks up the hat to see, quickly pick up the drink and guzzle it down, after he has removed the hat.

BIG BLUE BAMBOOZLE

Betcha you can't jump over a straw that I will place on the floor.

Place the straw against the wall.

Betcha I can balance a glass of water on a nickel.

Use a flat-bottomed glass and a buffalo nickel *(not too worn)*, and, filling the glass one-third with water, balance the glass between the word *liberty* and the edge of the Indian's nose. *Tip* the glass slightly till balanced, then remove hands. (Be sure to be ready if the glass starts to fall.)

Using three dice of equal size, bet the unwary that you can balance two dice on top of the third one, but he cannot.

After he has tried and failed, secretly moisten your thumb and place the moist part against one die, and abut it to the other dice. *Squeeze* the dice so that they adhere (due to the wetness in between) and carefully place them atop the single die.

BAR BETCHAS

Betcha can't make a die stand on its corner.

Place the corner of one die into the center dot of the three spot on another die.

Bet that you can drop a coin into a bottle without touching it.

Snap a wooden match in the middle, being careful not to break it in two. Place it across the mouth of a bottle and place a small coin on top of it. (See below). The bottle neck must be big enough that the coin will drop into it and yet small enough that the match will not. Allow a large drop of water to fall upon the broken joint of the match. The wood fibers will swell and straighten out, allowing the coin to drop into the bottle.

BAR BETCHAS

Five glasses are standing in a row . . . one and two are empty; three, four, and five are full. Betcha you can't, in one move, make the order "one full, two empty, three full, four empty, and the fifth glass full."

> If you will pour glass four into glass one and replace it in line, you will have the above setup.

Betcha I can cross the length of the bar, down my drink, and return to the other end of the bar in one second.

> Take out your watch, and when one second has ticked off, cross over to your drink and leisurely toss it down and return to the other end of the bar.

BIG BLUE BAMBOOZLE

Betcha can't transfer whiskey from one shot glass to another shot glass full of water, and vice versa, without using another container.

Place a business card on top of the glass with the water. Turn upside down and place on top of the whiskey. Pull the card slightly to one side, and the two liquids will exchange places.

From a lamp or from a fixture, hang a cup on a string. Bet that you can cut the string and the cup will remain hanging.

> Tie a loop and knot in the string while the cup is hanging. Then cut off the loop. The cup will remain suspended.

7

Magic—With Cards, Cups, Cigarettes, Coins, and Matches

After shuffling a deck of cards, ask a spectator to name any two cards (not their suits) and bet him that they will be together somewhere in the deck together.

> It's in the cards, and the odds are with you that you will be correct.

Betcha I can push a coin through a ring. (Use a quarter.)

> Put your finger through the ring and push the quarter.

Betcha I can produce a rabbit anytime you want to see it.

Remove your hat, or a portion of your shirt—and show a little hair *(hare)*.

Divide a pack of cards into two heaps, face down. Then you say: "I bet you will turn over a picture card before I do." You both turn a card over, one at a time.

If he comes to a picture card first, then you win. If you come to a picture first, you will put it on the side, face down. Of course, he will get suspicious and will turn it face up. That makes you win, as he turned the card over first.

Betcha I can hand you any card you think of in this well-shuffled deck of cards.

Keep handing him one card at a time, until the deck is entirely in his hands. Naturally, when he has the entire pack in his hands, his card is among them.

MAGIC

Place a spool of thread in your jacket handkerchief pocket, and with a needle allow about an inch to come through the jacket. Ask the poor lad to kindly remove the little piece of thread.

> The thread will continually unravel in your pocket until he gets wise.

Place a coin on a table and cover it with a Dixie cup. Then place a handkerchief over the cup. Then bet that you can remove the coin without touching the cup or the hanky.

> Wave your hands mystically and say a few magic words. Tell your friend that it is done and tell him to look and see. When he removes the hanky and cup, you remove the coin.

Betcha I can put this die on the table so that when you roll two more dice, the total of any two or all three will be seven.

> Set it with the 1 up. The odds are five out of nine you will win.

Shuffle a deck. Ask someone to call out any two cards whose sum is thirteen. (Picture cards count as ten). Show the first three cards. If neither of these three cards is one of the selected cards, you can almost safely predict that the two selected cards will be found adjacent in the pack.

The law of averages is in your favor.

Here is an excellent trick at your dinner table. The magician takes his glass tumbler half full of water. He tilts this glass on his table and it stands quite a long time (as long as he wishes). Then he picks up the glass, drinks its contents, and leaves it aside.

The *secret* is a small piece of matchstick which was previously kept concealed under the tablecloth. Even a piece from ordinary matchsticks, say a quarter of an inch long, will be enough. As the glass bottom is pushed against this tiny piece of wood, it will be found by experiment that there is enough support to keep the glass in balancing position. It is better

MAGIC

to have the glass half filled with water as in that case the act of balancing will be easy. It is difficult to perform the trick with an empty glass.

Hold a box of wooden matches about a foot above the table. When you let go, the box falls on one end and remains standing. When someone else tries it, the box always falls over.

Secret: Before you drop the box, see that the drawer projects upward a half inch from the box. Your hand hides this. When the box lands, inertia makes the drawer slide quickly into the box. This prevents the box from bouncing and landing on its side.

Can you spin an egg, bring it to a dead stop with your finger, then cause it to start spinning again without touching it in any way?

Spin the egg on a plate, then stop it suddenly by placing the tip of your finger on top. Immediately lift your finger. The egg will start spinning slowly. Although you bring the shell to a stop, the inside keeps on going. So, when you lift your finger, it starts the egg turning.

BIG BLUE BAMBOOZLE

Claiming to be a big ESP expert, ask someone to write something on a piece of paper and cover it up with his hand.

Then bet that you can tell him what's on the paper... *his hand*.

A man can be lifted with five fingers. Here's how:

One person places a finger under his shoe. Another person places a finger under his other shoe. A third person places a finger under his elbow. A fourth person places a finger under his other elbow. A fifth person places a finger under his chin. *Now*—all lift at once, and he can be raised at least two feet off the floor.

Challenge your friend to make a wooden match stand upright. When he fails, you secretly wet the end of the match with your finger. It will stand.

MAGIC

You cannot make a circle with a dot in the center without taking the pencil off the paper.

Fold the corner, begin at dot.

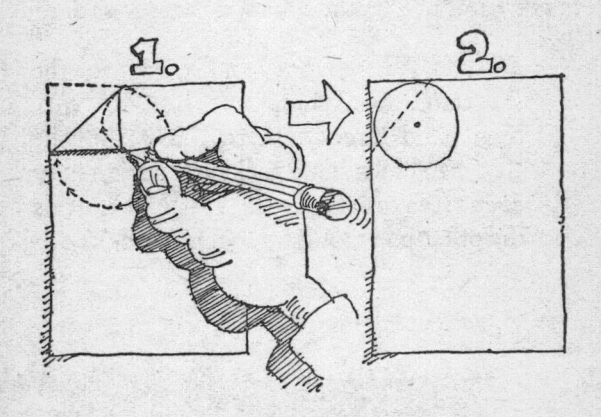

This trick will fool them, but never repeat it before the same audience. *Effect:* Magician hands cards from an ordinary deck to spectator, saying, "I am going to hand you cards, two at a time, and I want you to make two even piles. Then I will hand one card and you make whichever pile you wish—odd."

When this is done, magician says, "Pick up the odd pile and hand me two cards at a time, but keep the odd card." Spectator finds to his astonishment that the pile he thought was odd is *even* and pile he thought was even is *odd*.

> *Secret:* When you hand cards to the spectator, hand him nine sets of twos, then hand him *one* card. Now the pile that he thinks he is making odd is really *even* (ten cards are in that pile). It is the other pile that is odd (nine cards).

Lay out three rows of matches; you can take one match or whole row. Person taking last match is loser.

MAGIC

The following can't be done no matter how hard you try:

Take any playing card, bend it about one-half to three-quarters of an inch from the edge on both sides and stand it up in this position. No matter how hard you blow, the card will remain standing on its two "legs."

Betcha I can name the first card you turn over when you return to this room. You can even shuffle the deck before you leave the room.

Lean the card against the door through which the person will reenter the room.

8
Mathematics—Betchas Using Numbers

Isn't it amazing how mathematics is tied into everything—nature, music, biology. Everything in this world seems to follow certain mathematical patterns.

Each day a bus leaves Detroit for Chicago at 8:00 A.M., and a bus leaves Chicago for Detroit at 8:30 A.M. Betcha don't know which bus is closer to Detroit when the two meet.

> When the two buses meet, they are the same distance from Detroit as well as from Chicago.

There were seven men in a rowboat. They had eight cigarettes but no matches. Betcha don't know how they lit their cigarettes.

> They threw one cigarette overboard and made their boat a cigarette lighter.

Betcha can't write eleven thousand, eleven hundred and eleven correctly the first time.

    12,111.

Betcha don't know which is correct: Seven plus nine is fifteen; or, seven plus nine are fifteen.

    Neither; seven plus nine is sixteen.

Betcha I can take four from four and leave eight.

    Take a square piece of paper and tear off the four corners. You will end up with eight corners.

Betcha don't know if it's possible to carry water across the room in a sieve.

    Only if it's in the form of ice cubes.

MATHEMATICS

If there were ten candles burning at the same time, and I blew four of them out, betcha can't tell me how many candles would be left.

> *Four* . . . since the rest were left lit, they would burn down.

Betcha don't know how much sand there is in a hole in the ground whose dimensions are two inches long, two inches deep, and two inches wide.

> None.

Betcha I can pick up four matches from a plate, using only four matches, one at a time, and yet leave one match on the plate.

> Remove three matches from the plate one at a time and then pick up the plate with the last match still on the plate.

A bottle and a cork cost three cents. The bottle costs one cent more than the cork. How much does each cost?

> Bottle—two cents.
> Cork—one cent.

Ask a friend of yours to play a simple game of chance with you. Take sixteen cards—the four aces, twos, threes, and fours—and arrange them in a rectangle so that at the top you have the aces (each counting one), then the twos, etc. Alternately, each of you will turn one of the cards face down and will note its value. The one who reaches twenty-two first or compels his partner to go beyond that mark has won. There is a method by which you can always win, provided you turn the first card. How?

> You can win (or, rather, must win) unless you make a mistake. If you can, reach seven, twelve, or seventeen. You will be sure to reach one of these marks only if you start with one, though there remains a slight chance if you begin with two. In all other cases, your friend can easily reach seven, twelve, or seventeen and he may win.

MATHEMATICS

Ten men come to a motel that has only nine rooms in it and they all insist on sleeping there that night. If you were the owner of the motel how would you accommodate them without having two men sleep in the same room?

This is the floor plan for the motel:

Now, place guests 1 and 2 in room A; 3 in B; 4 in C; 5 in D; 6 in E; 7 in F; 8 in G; 9 in H; and the extra in A, 2 (who is the tenth man) in I and you have solved the problem.

BIG BLUE BAMBOOZLE

Freddy the frog falls into a ninety-nine foot well with a great splash and at once starts climbing to the top. He goes up three feet every day and falls back two each night. Freddy continues in this indomitable fashion until he has reached the very top of the well. How long has it taken him?

99 days

Find the Heads—The magician borrows a box of matches, looks at it for a moment, then lays it on the table and designates one end to be the heads. When the box is opened, the heads are seen to be at the end designated by the magician.

> *Secret:* Momentarily balance the box horizontally on your forefinger long enough for you to notice which way the box topples. That will be the end of the box where the heads lie; for the heads are heavier than the other ends of the matches.

Smash It—Remove the matchbox drawer; set the cover on its side, and place the drawer on end upon the side of the cover. Now ask some powerful person to smash the drawer and the cover with a blow of his fist.

The harder he strikes, the less chance he has of success. The cover and the drawer will fly away from his hand as soon as he strikes them.

Striking Safety Matches—Nonchalantly strike a safety match on the sole of your shoe. People who attempt to duplicate the feat are always unsuccessful.

Secret: Beforehand, rub the side of a matchbox against the instep of your shoe. Some of the striking substance will be transferred from the box to your shoe, and it will be a simple matter for you to strike a match there.

Picking Up the Drawer—Lay the drawer of a matchbox upside down upon the table and set the cover on end upon it. The trick is to pick up the cover and lift the drawer with it . . . without touching the drawer.

Secret: To do this one, place your lips to the upper end of the cover and lift it, at the same time drawing your breath. The suction will lift the drawer also.

BIG BLUE BAMBOOZLE

The Box on the Door—A borrowed matchbox is set against the end of a door, and it hangs there half opened and full of matches, just as though it were on a holder. This is accomplished by pushing the box up along the door.

> After two or three pushes, the matchbox will stick in place—sometimes so firmly that a match may be struck upon the side of it. Use safety matches.

Label Up—Toss a box of matches in the air. It falls with the label side up. Every time the box is spun, it falls the same way. Simply insert a coin—a quarter or a half dollar—under the drawer of the matchbox. It adds weight to the bottom of the box, so that when the box is whirled in the air it will always come with the bottom down.

Betcha don't know what's a Gazinta?

> Two gazinta four twice; three gazinta six twice.

MATHEMATICS

What number would revive a lady who fainted?

> Bring her 2.

What's the difference between 100 and 1,000?

> 0.

Betcha can't add two numbers to 19, the sum being less than 20.

> ½.

How much is 25 × 3 × 0?

> 0.

Three times what number equals four times the same number?

> 0.

Betcha in a field of four hundred sheep, three shepherds, two horses, and four dogs, you can't tell me how many feet can you count?

> Ans: Six feet—the other are hooves and paws.

Why did the teacher mark "underwater" to fail Johnny on his test?

    Because underwater is below "C" level.

If a butcher is six feet two inches tall, what does he weigh?

    Meat.

How many feet in a yard?

    Depends on how many people are standing there.

How can you divide four apples among three people?

    Make applesauce.

What do you get when you tear a piece of paper in half, in half again, and in half again.

    Confetti.

When do 2 and 3 equal more than 5?

    When it's 23.

MATHEMATICS

How many times can you take ten from one hundred?
> Only once—every other subtraction is from a smaller number.

What's a polygon?
> A dead poly.

What can be right but never wrong?
> An angle.

What's the point of studying mathematics?
> Decimal point.

What's bought by the yard and worn by the foot?
> A rug.

When does a bicycle go as fast as an airplane?
> When it's in an airplane.

What number is a dangerous one?

>   Fore.

Bet you can't use the number 2 to describe your vacation.

>   A vacation is 2 weeks that are 2 short, after which you're 2 tired 2 go home and 2 broke not 2.

What's the right angle to approach a problem?

>   The *try*angle.

What can you always count on?

>   Your fingers.

If a barrel weighed twenty pounds—what would you fill it with to make it eighteen pounds?

>   Holes.

9
Betcha Riddles and Conundrums

Riddles are one-line challenges or betchas and as such can, by proper solution, be used endlessly. Finding answers to riddles requires mental agility. Riddles prepare the mind and make it alert and active for anything that it might be called upon to perform in the future.

Riddles give quickness and facility for turning a problem about in many ways and viewing it in every possible light. Finding answers to riddles is the same kind of exercise for the mind as running, leaping, and dancing are for the body.

Riddles can be divided into different types, though some will fall into more than one category. Some riddles are asked as if they were *serious problems,* or betchas.

Q: If you were to throw a stone into the Red Sea, what would it become?

A: Wet.

Q: What goes around the house without legs?

A: A broom.

Q: What room can no one enter?

A: A mushroom.

Q: Which is heavier? A pound of gold or a pound of feathers?

A: Feathers weigh a pound avoirdupois (sixteen ounces). Gold weighs a pound troy (twelve ounces).

Q: Why is eternity like a circle?
A: Because there is no end.

Q: Why is a watch like a river?
A: Because it doesn't run long without winding.

Q: When is a door not a door?
A: When it is ajar.

Q: When is a lamp not a lamp?
A: When it's alight.

Q: When is a boy not a boy?
A: When he is a shaver.

Q: When did Moses sleep five in a bed?
A: When he slept with his forefathers.

Q: How long did Caine hate his brother?
A: As long as he was Abel.

Q: Why do you look over a stone wall?
A: Because you can't look through it.

Q: When will water stop running downhill?
A: When it reaches the bottom.

Q: When does a chair dislike you?
A: When it can no longer bear you.

Q: How can you make a slow horse fast?
A: Stop feeding him.

Q: What animal keeps the best time?
A: A watchdog.

BETCHA RIDDLES AND CONUNDRUMS

Q: Why are the tallest people the laziest?

A: Because they are longer in bed than others.

Q: Where do you go on your fourteenth birthday?

A: Into your fifteenth year.

Q: What has four I's and can't see?

A: Mississippi

Q: What smells most in a drugstore?

A: Your nose.

Q: What are the most difficult ships to conquer?

A: Hardships.

Q: What is the first thing a man sets in his garden?
A: His foot.

Q: Which is the left side of a chocolate cake?
A: The part that is not eaten.

Q: What is more wonderful than a horse that can count?
A: A bee that can spell (spelling bee).

Q: What bird is rude?
A: A mocking bird.

Q: What can turn without moving?
A: An egg.

Q: What is the difference between a hill and a pill?

A: One is hard to get up and the other is hard to get down.

Q: What has neither flesh nor bone but has four fingers and a thumb?

A: A glove.

Q: What is the best way to make a fire with two sticks?

A: Make sure one of the sticks is a match.

Q: What did the big firecracker say to the little firecracker?

A: My pop is bigger than your pop.

Q: For what man should you always take off your hat?
A: The barber.

Q: What is an effective way of removing a cinder?
A: Take out the eye and wipe it with a damp towel.

Q: What is the best way to keep a skunk from smelling?
A: Hold his nose.

Q: What is white, has just one horn, and gives milk?
A: A milk truck.

Q: What is the best way to catch a fish?
A: Have someone throw it to you.

Q: What comes all the way to a house but never gets in?

A: The steps.

Q: What can fall down but never get hurt?

A: Snow.

Q: What kind of coat should be put on when it is wet?

A: A coat of paint.

Q: In what two professions is graft legal?

A: Tree surgery and operative surgery.

Q: Do they have a Fourth of July in England?

A: Yes, it is the day after the third of July.

Q: What has four wheels and flies?

A: A garbage truck.

Q: If a man is living in Winston-Salem, North Carolina, can he be buried west of the Mississippi?

A: Not if he's living.

Q: What is it that Adam didn't have yet gave to his children?

A: A father.

Q: A beggar's brother died, but the man who died had no brother. How is this possible?

A: The beggar was a woman.

Q: Can you hang a man in Texas with a wooden leg?

A: They usually hang a man with a rope.

Q: I have two coins in my hand totaling fifty-five cents in value. One is not a nickel. Explain.

A: The other one is.

Q: Two men played checkers. Each one won five games yet lost none. Explain.

A: They did not play each other.

Q: What runs but never moves?

A: A clock.

Q: What is it that the more you take from it, the bigger it gets?

A: A hole.

Q: Name a car that starts with P.

A: They all start with gas.

CONUNDRUMS

A conundrum is a riddle put in the form of an enigma or a puzzle. The answer usually depends upon a pun. They are generally questions that depend upon puns for effect.

Q: When is a sick man a contradiction?

A: When he is an impatient patient.

Q: Why should you be careful about telling secrets in the country?

A: Because the corn has ears, the potatoes have eyes, and the beans talk (beanstalk).

Q: What is the difference between a cloud and a boy getting a spanking?

A: The cloud pours with rain and boy roars with pain.

Q: What has three keys, has legs, but won't open doors?

A: Mon*keys*, don*keys*, and tur*keys*.

Q: Why is a traffic cop the strongest man in the world?

A: Because he can hold up a ten-ton truck with one hand.

Q: When does a ship tell a falsehood?

A: When she lies at wharf.

Q: Why was the little strawberry upset?

A: Because his ma and pa were in a jam.

Q: What is the difference between a sailor and six broken clocks?

A: The sailor goes to see, and the clocks cease to go.

Q: What is the difference between a book of fiction and the rear light of a car?

A: One is a light tale, and the other is a tail light.

Q: What is the difference between a mirror and a chatterbox?

A: A mirror reflects without speaking; A chatterbox speaks without reflecting.

Q: What is the difference between a teacher and a train?

A: The teacher says: "Spit out that gum!" The train says: "Chew, chew, chew!" ("Choo, choo, choo.")

Q: Why is a schoolteacher like a railroad conductor?

A: One minds the train and other trains the mind.

Q: What is the difference between a beautiful girl and a mouse?

A: The mouse harms the cheese; the girl charms the he's.

Q: Why is a man who is always complaining the easiest man to satisfy?

A: Because *nothing* satisfies him.

Q: Why is a caterpillar like a hot biscuit?

A: Because it makes the butterfly.

Q: Why is a fly one of the grocer's best customers?

A: Because when the fly comes for sugar, he settles on the spot.

Q: When does a caterpillar improve its morals?

A: When it turns over a new leaf.

Q: What is the difference between a cat and a frog?

A: The cat has only nine lives; a frog croaks every minute.

Q: When is a frog unable to talk?

A: When he's got a man in his throat.

Q: What did the nearsighted porcupine say when it backed into a cactus?

A: "Pardon me, honey."

Q: Why does a stork stand on one leg?

A: Because if he took two legs off the ground, he would fall down.

Q: What is the difference between perseverance and obstinacy?

A: One arises from a strong "will," and the other from a strong "won't."

Q: What is the difference between photographers and whooping cough?

A: One makes facsimiles, and the other makes sick families.

Q: What is the difference between the manager of a theater and a sailor?

A: A sailor likes to see a lighthouse and the manager likes to see a full house.

Q: What is the difference between a postage stamp and a mule?

A: One you stick with a lick and the other you lick with a stick.

Q: What is the difference between a primitive man and a modern man?

A: When a modern man's wife talks too much, he goes to his Club; the primitive man reached for his club.

Q: What is the difference between a man who has eaten a hearty meal and a man who has signed his will?

A: One is dined and sated, the other is signed and dated.

Q: What is the difference between a crazy hare and a counterfeit coin?

A: One is mad bunny, and the other is bad money.

Q: What is the favorite word with women?

A: The last one.

Q: What do you break when you move it?

A: Silence.

Q: What is that which you can keep even after you have given it to someone else?

A: Your word.

Q: What is the longest word in the English language?

A: *Smiles*—because it has a mile between the first and last letters.

Q: What letter placed in front of the word *laughter* will make a new word which completely changes the meaning and pronunciation of the word?

A: The letter *s*—slaughter.

Q: What word is made shorter by adding a syllable to it?

A: The word *short*—the syllable *er* shorter.

Q: If a pencil and a piece of paper had a race, which would win?

A: The pencil—because the paper would always remain stationary (stationery).

Q: What is the difference between a girl and a stamp?

A: One is a female, the other is the mail fee.

Q: What odd number when beheaded becomes even?

A: Seven.

Q: Take two letters away from what four-letter word and have four left?

A: From *five* take F and E, leaving IV (four).

Q: Why is an author more than a king?

A: He may choose his own subjects.

Q: If all the letters in the alphabet were on a mountain top, which letter would leave first?

A: *D* would begin the descent.

Q: Why is a teacher of girls like the letter *c*?

A: She makes lasses into classes.

Q: What letter travels the greatest distance?

A: *D*, because it goes to the end of the world.

Q: Why are the abbreviations of degrees tacked on to a man's name?

A: To show that he is a man of letters.

Q: A word therein five syllables contains—Take one away—not one of them remains.

A: Monosyllable. Take "mo" and leave "*no syllable.*"

BIG BLUE BAMBOOZLE

Q: Why is the letter *a* like noon?
A: Because it's the middle of the d*a*y.

Q: Spell black water in three letters.
A: I-n-k.

Q: What word of three letters has six left after you take two away?
A: S-i-x-t-y.

Q: Spell hard water in three letters.
A: I-c-e.

Q: Spell dried grass in three letters.
A: H-a-y.

Q: Why is the A like honeysuckle?

A: Because it always has a B following it.

Q: Why did Noah object to the letter *d*?

A: Because it made the Ark dark.

Q: What's in the church but not the steeple?

A: The parson has it, but not the people—the letter *r*.

Q: What is it that occurs once in a minute, twice in a moment, and not once in a thousand years?

A: The letter m.

BIG BLUE BAMBOOZLE

Q: What was it that Queen Mary had before and King William had behind and Queen Anne did not have at all?

A: The letter *m*.

Q: What is it from which the whole may be taken and yet some will remain?

A: The word *wholesome*.

Q: What word of only three syllables contains twenty-six letters?

A: The alphabet.

Q: Why is a dog's tail like the heart of a tree?

A: Because it's farthest from the bark.

Q: What is that which no man wishes to have yet no man would wish to lose?

A: A bald head.

Q: What has four legs and flies?

A: A dead horse, or two pairs of pants.

Q: Why is a dirty child like flannel?

A: Because it shrinks from washing.

Q: What part of a fish is like the end of a book?

A: Why, the finis!

Q: What word is composed of five letters from which, if you take two, one remains?

A: Stone (one).

Q: Why is the letter *y* like a young spendthrift?

A: Because he makes Pa pay.

Q: What ships hardly ever sail out of sight?

A: Hardships.

Q: What motive led to the invention of the railroad?

A: The locomotive.

Q: Why are deaf people like Dutch cheeses?

A: Because you can't make them here.

Q: Why was the first day of Adam's life the longest?

A: Because it had no *Eve*.

Q: How much is four plus three? Five plus two? Six plus one? How many weeks in a day?
A: Weeks in a day?

Q: When can you jump while you're sitting down?
A: When playing checkers.

Q: What makes a road broad?
A: The letter *b*.

Q: What makes a coat last?
A: When you make the pants first.

Q: What's the definition of a synonym?
A: A word used when you can't spell the word you want.

BIG BLUE BAMBOOZLE

Q: Four men build four boats in four days. How long will it take one man to build one boat?

A: Four days.

Q: When is a hinge needed and loving?

A: When it's something to *adore*.

Q: An expert skier dreamed he was on a skiing trip with his wife and mother (long sad story). Betcha I can give the skier two words that will solve his problem immediately.

A: *Wake up!*

Q: What is the best paper for making kites?

A: *Fly* paper.

Q: When does a man wear a large watch?

A: When he expects to have a *big* time.

Q: What kind of dress lasts longest?

A: A house dress, because it is never worn *out*.

Q: When is soup sure to run out of the bowl?

A: When there is a *leak* in it.

Q: What part of a watch has been used before?

A: The second hand.

Q: Why was the little drop of cider so sad?

A: Because all his friends were in the jug.

Q: Why is a sick boy improved when he makes a bet of five cents?

A: Because it makes him a little *better*.

Q: What was Joan of Arc made of?

A: She was *maid* of Orleans.

Q: Why is the interior of a theater such a sad place?

A: Because all the seats are in *tiers*.

Q: How can you leave the room with two legs and come back with six?

A: Come back carrying a chair.

Q: Why is a pig in the parlor like a house on fire?

A: Because the sooner it's put out, the better.

Q: Why is a wise man like a pin?
A: Because he has a head and comes to the point.

Q: What's put on the table and cut but never eaten?
A: A pack of cards.

Q: Why do some carpenters reasonably believe there's no such a thing as stone?
A: Because they never *saw* it.

Q: Why does a duck go into water?
A: Because of *divers* reasons.

Q: What lives on its own substance and dies when it has devoured itself?
A: A fire.

Sometimes riddles are not intended to be answered, but merely offer opportunities for "wisecracks" or clever statements.

Q: Who was the fastest runner in history?

A: Adam—he was the first in the human race.

Q: At what time was Adam born?

A: A little before *Eve*.

Q: Why are you always so tired on April Fool's Day?

A: Because you have just finished a March of thirty-one days.

Q: Why does a train never sit down?
A: Because it has a tender behind.

Q: Why isn't your nose twelve inches long?
A: Because then it would be a foot.

Q: What animal changes his size twice every day?
A: A dog—because you let him out every night and take him in every morning.

Q: Why are the people in Ireland the richest in the world?
A: Because their *capital* is always *Dublin*.

Q: If a girl falls down, why can't her brother help her to her feet?
A: How can he be a brother and assist her too?

Q: What is it that goes around a button?

A: A goat goes around a-*buttin'*.

Q: When is a doctor most annoyed?

A: When he is out of patien*t*s.

Q: What belongs to you but is used more by your friends than by yourself?

A: Your name.

Q: When does a man have four hands?

A: When he doubles his fists.

Q: What is the keynote of good manners?

A: B natural.

Q: Which animal took most luggage into the Ark, and which took the least?

A: The elephant took the most, for he carried his trunk, while the fox and the cock had only a brush and a comb between them.

Q: Who is the silliest mother you ever heard of?

A: Mother Goose.

Q: Where was King George crowned?

A: On his head.

Q: Where was Moses when the lights when out?

A: In the dark.

Q: When Washington crossed the Delaware, what did he see on his left hand?

A: He saw five fingers.

Q: How many famous men have been born in a small town?

A: None. Only babies are born.

Q: Where did Noah strike the first nail he put in the Ark?

A: On the head.

Q: What is the difference between an old dime and a new nickel?

A: Five cents.

Q: Can you jump higher than a six-foot wall?

A: Yes! Walls cannot jump.

Q: What is it that goes from New York to Florida without moving?

A: The road.

Q: What four letters frighten a thief?

A: O I C U.

Q: What's the smallest bridge in the world?

A: The bridge on your nose.

Q: Why are teeth like verbs?

A: Because they are regular, irregular, and defective.

Q: Why is a shoemaker a most industrious man?

A: Because he works to the last.

Q: Why is the Isthmus of Suez like the first *u* in "cucumber"?

A: Because it's between two *c*'s (seas).

Q: Why is sympathy like blindman's bluff?

A: Because it's a fellow feeling for a fellow creature.

Q: What plant stands for 4?

A: IV (ivy).

Q: What is it that never asks questions and yet requires many answers?

A: The doorbell.

Q: Why is it probably that beer was made in the Ark?

A: Because the kangaroo went in with the hops, and the bear was always *bruin*.

Q: Why does an Indian with pigtails wear a sweater?

A: Because he feels cold.

Q: What was the president's name twenty years ago?

A: The same as it is today.

Q: What's the greatest number of players that can legitimately be on a baseball field at one time?

A: Thirteen . . . nine on team, three on bases, and the batter up.

Q: Which is heavier—a half moon or a full moon?

A: A half moon—because the full moon is *lighter*.

Q: Which is the oldest tree?

A: The elder.

Q: Why do potatoes grow better than other vegetables?

A: Because they have eyes to see what they're doing.

Q: What man in the Bible was the busiest doctor?

A: Job—he had more patien*ce* than anybody.

Q: Which bird can lift the heaviest weights?

A: The *crane*.

Q: What thing is it that is lower with a head than without one?

A: A pillow.

Q: If a man who is carrying a dozen glass lamps drops one, what does he become?

A: A lamp lighter.

Q: Why is a dog biting his tail a good manager?

A: Because he makes both ends meet.

Q: Why is a fish monger never generous?

A: Because his business makes him sell fish (selfish).

Q: Why is it that a tailor won't attend to business?

A: Because he is always cutting out.

Q: Why were gloves never meant to sell?

A: Because they were made to be kept on hand.

10

Oddities and Novelties—Betchas Using Everyday Articles

Bet a man that a woman can perform a simple task that a man cannot do. Then ask him to face the wall and take two steps back from the wall. Place a chair before him; as he places his head against the wall, ask him to try to raise the chair. To his surprise, he will not be able to do so.

A woman, because of the body displacement, will find this to be an easy task.

Betcha don't know how to make a Venetian blind.

Poke his eyes out.

Some months have thirty-one days, some have only thirty. Betcha can't tell me how many months have twenty-eight days?

All of them.

Bet a person that the Constitution specifies four requirements for becoming president of the United States. He has to be at least thirty-five years old, born a citizen, and must have lived in the country at least fourteen years. What is the fourth?

He must first be elected.

Bet a person that you can make four different sounds just by blowing through a straw, and not using any voice at all. He cannot.

Make two cuts on the end of the straw to form a point. Then blow through the straw (like a reed). As the sound is emitted, cut off an inch from the end of the straw and blow again, and repeat this twice more. Each time, another sound will be heard.

ODDITIES AND NOVELTIES

Bet that you can pick up an ice cube from a glass of water by using just a piece of string.

> Using a light cotton string, allow a portion of it to lie upon the ice cube. In a while the string will be frozen to the cube. You may then lift the cube out of the glass.

Bet that no one can name the president whose picture is on a ten-dollar bill.

> Hamilton was never president.

Name the current president of the United States. Now bet that they cannot tell you who the treasurer is.

> Look at the name on a one-dollar bill.

Obtain a pack of Camel cigarettes and bet that your victim cannot count correctly the number of *es* on the back of the pack.

> After he arrives at the answer, have him again count the *es* from the bottom *up*. His answer will be different.

BIG BLUE BAMBOOZLE

Bet that he can't read the following sentences correctly out loud:

Paris	Birds	Once
In The	In The	In A
Spring	Hand	Lifetime

I bet that *you* don't know—how many *two*-cent stamps in a dozen?

> There are twelve two-cent stamps in a dozen.

Bet that you can float a pin in a glass of water.

> Place a piece of paper napkin on the surface and place the pin on top. It will float.

ODDITIES AND NOVELTIES

Betcha I can turn an egg completely around in an egg cup without touching the egg.

>Place the egg in an old-fashioned egg cup. Then blow down strongly between the egg and the cup (which causes the air to raise the egg from the cup.) Then slowly turn the cup as you continue blowing.

Bet that I can drop a lump of sugar into a cup of coffee without wetting the sugar.

>Use powdered coffee.

Betcha I can remove an object and you can't replace it the same way I removed it.

>Twist off a salt-shaker cap. It comes off counterclockwise; he has to replace it *clockwise*.

Have a person stretch out his arms parallel to the floor. Place a book in each hand and bet him that he cannot transfer the books without bending his arms or shoulders or elbows.

    Lay the books down, turn around, and pick up the books again.

Bet you don't know the capital of Florida.

    Capital *F*.

A owns a peacock. If the peacock lays an egg in *B*'s yard, who owns the egg?

    Peacocks do not lay eggs.

ODDITIES AND NOVELTIES

Bet that you can distribute ten pieces of sugar into three cups so that every cup contains an odd number of pieces.

> Take seven pieces of sugar and place them in one cup and place three pieces in another cup. Finally, take any one of these cups and place it in the empty cup.

Wager someone that you can light a candle, blow it out, and relight it without applying a match to it.

> First light the candle and blow it out. Put the still-lit match about two inches above the candle. The rising smoke, containing carbon, should ignite the candle as the flame burns down the carbon stream.

Betcha can't light twenty matches in a row without missing a strike.

> It's a rarity, as the phosphorus wears out and makes the striking surface worn.

Betcha don't know why a barber in Geneva would rather cut the hair of two Frenchmen than one German.

>Because he makes twice as much money.

Bet you can't place a mathematical symbol between 2 and 3 to express a number greater than 2 and less than 3.

>2.3.

Betcha can't tell me why manhole covers are round.

>If a square cover were turned on its edge, it could slip through and fall into the sewer.

ODDITIES AND NOVELTIES

Betcha you can't tell what three positive integers have a sum equal to their product.

$1 \times 2 \times 3$.

Betcha can't tell the difference between an apple and an onion.

Close your eyes, hold your nose, and taste each one.

Bet that I can separate your closed fists with one blow of my forefingers, while you can't separate mine.

Hit his fists away from each other. When you put your fists together, put your lower thumb into the upper fist.

Bet that if you went to bed at eight o'clock at night, and set the alarm to get up at nine o'clock in the morning, he couldn't tell how many hours of sleep this would permit.

> One hour.

Betcha I can boil water in a paper cup.

> Take a small amount of water in a paper cup and hold a match under it. The water will carry away the heat of the flame so the cup won't burn.

What's the area of a triangle with a ten-inch base, one side six inches, and the other side three inches? Wanna bet?

> Can't be a triangle with those dimensions.

ODDITIES AND NOVELTIES

Betcha can't say how long they would last if a doctor gave you three pills and told you to take one every half hour.

One hour.

Betcha can't separate a mixture of salt and pepper in this mixed-up pile, and I can.

Run a plastic comb through your hair; then hold it near the pile, and the pepper will jump out of the pile and cling to the comb.

Bet you can't tell which letters are missing from the phone dial.

Q and Z.

BIG BLUE BAMBOOZLE

Bet you can't tell me correctly what letter is in the first hole of the dial phone.

> None; just the digit 1.

Bet I can guess whether the first chapter of any book starts on an even or odd page, if you tell me the name of the author or the publisher.

> The first chapter always starts on the right-hand page—odd number.

Betcha you can't tell how many kings there are in a deck of cards.

> Five . . . most jokers have a king riding a bike.

ODDITIES AND NOVELTIES

Betcha in a group of a dozen or more, two people will pick the same card; have the same change in their pockets; their father or mother's name will be the same; have the same birthday; and two license plates out of twenty will have the same last two digits.

Statistics prove this.

Divide thirty by one-half and add ten. Bet you can't give me the correct answer the first time.

Seventy (didn't say divide by two.)

If you take two apples from three apples, how many do you have?

Want to bet it's two apples?

BIG BLUE BAMBOOZLE

Place six cards down on a table face down. If there are only two kings in the packet, you can safely bet, two to one, that if three cards are turned over, one will be a king.

Try it.

All banknotes have eight digits in their serial number ... it's safe to bet that he can't name three numbers on the bill, given only one try.

It's odd but usually true. Cover a bill with your hand and see for yourself.

Have you ever seen a photo of Benjamin Franklin?

There was no photography in his time.

Did Columbus view America or Cuba with his spy glass?

    The spy glass was not invented yet.

Did Julius Caesar ever make a pipe?

    Tobacco had not yet been discovered.

If your neighbor's rooster lays an egg in your backyard, to whom does the egg belong?

    A rooster lays an egg?

A chemist invented a liquid that can dissolve anything and has a bottleful.

    The bottle would then be dissolved.

If a cantaloupe fell off a nine foot tree, how far down the hill would it roll if the hill was sixty-two feet long?

    Cantaloupes don't grow on trees.

What has three eyes, twenty-four legs, twelve with hair, six toes on each leg, and turns from white to red to green when frightened?

    Nothing.

What word has
only vowels?　　　　(Aye)

What word has five
*a*s and no other
vowel?　　　　(Abracadabra)

ODDITIES AND NOVELTIES

What word has six *I*s? (Indivisibility)

What sense has no meaning? (Nonsense)

What do you have that's easiest to part with? (Comb)

What word is pronounced differently when capitalized? (Polish and polish)

What must a girl do to have soft hands? (Nothing)

How can you get
 down from an
 elephant?

(You can't. You
 get down from
 a goose.)

Why did Robin
 Hood rob the
 rich and give
 to the poor?

(Because the poor
 had no money.)

How can you
 double your
 money

(Fold it.)

Here are 9 wacky, zany, all-in-good-fun, two-in-one joke books from ace comedian, Larry Wilde

Order the ones you want today!

___ OFFICIAL BLACK FOLKS/ WHITE FOLKS JOKE BOOK	P722	$1.25
___ OFFICIAL DEMOCRAT/ REPUBLICAN JOKE BOOK	P818	$1.25
___ OFFICIAL GOLFERS JOKE BOOK	P40-048	$1.50
___ OFFICIAL JEWISH/ IRISH JOKE BOOK	P320	$1.25
___ OFFICIAL POLISH/ ITALIAN JOKE BOOK	P548	$1.25
___ MORE OFFICIAL POLISH/ ITALIAN JOKE BOOK	P772	$1.25
___ OFFICIAL RELIGIOUS/ NOT SO RELIGIOUS JOKE BOOK	P904	$1.25
___ OFFICIAL SMART KIDS/ DUMB PARENTS JOKE BOOK	P40-011	$1.25
___ OFFICIAL VIRGINS/ SEX MANIACS JOKE BOOK	P634	$1.25

If you can't find these books at your local bookstore, simply send the cover price, plus 25¢ for postage and handling to:

Pinnacle Books
275 Madison Avenue, New York, New York 10016

DO YOU KNOW HOW TO . . . ?
(Pinnacle Books can help you)

Launch a new child star?
_____ THE SOLID GOLD SANDBOX, Jay Bonderoff — P774 1.50

Benefit from meditation?
_____ MEDITATION: A Step Beyond with Edgar Cayce — P547 1.25

Garden—dirt cheap!
_____ THE FREE EARTH GUIDE TO GARDENING, Kramer — P567 1.95

Get the most from your doctor's appointment?
_____ HOW TO HELP YOUR DOCTOR HELP YOU, Gaver — P587 1.75

Lose weight without counting calories?
_____ THE THIN BOOK, By a Formerly Fat Psychiatrist. Rubin, M.D. — P077 1.25

Stop those headaches!
_____ WHAT YOU CAN DO ABOUT YOUR HEADACHES. Hass, M.D. & Dolan — P301 .95

See tomorrow today?
_____ HOW TO TELL FORTUNES, Rod Davies — P793 1.25

Get the kinks out?
_____ ZONE THERAPY: Step by Step Guide to Applied Pressure Therapy, Anika Bergson & Vladimir Tuchak — P456 1.25

Use your mind to improve your health?
_____ PSYCHOSOMATICS (How Your Emotions Can Damage Your Health), H & M Lewis — P532 1.75

Become a complete person?
_____ BODYMIND (The Whole Person Health Book), Miller — P566 1.50

Be a full-fledged witch?
_____ CAST YOUR OWN SPELL, Sybil Leek — P656 1.25

YOU CAN ORDER ANY OF THESE BOOKS RIGHT HERE: Please add 25¢ per book for postage and handling up to $1.00—free thereafter.

Pinnacle Books
275 Madison Avenue
New York, N.Y. 10016

_____ Check here if you wish to receive our free catalog

PB-24

DO YOU KNOW HOW TO?

(Pinnacle does and can help you!)

Save gas! THE GAS SAVER'S GUIDE, Callender & Woods	P437	1.50
Defend yourself! (and stay trim with exercise) THE BEGINNER'S GUIDE TO KUNG-FU, Dennis & Simmons	P701	2.50
Look younger and feel younger? THE PURSUIT OF YOUTH, Rae Lindsay	P833	1.75
Read faster, think clearer, and express yourself better? SPEED-THINK, Hans Holzer	P919	1.50
Perform feats of magic? HOUDINI'S BOOK OF MAGIC TRICKS, PUZZLES & STUNTS, Harry Houdini	P970	1.50
Get rid of aches and pains? SHIATZU: Japanese Pressure Point Massage, Anika Bergson & Vladimir Tuchak	P916	1.50
Play bridge? (learn while you laugh!) BRIDGE IN THE FOURTH DIMENSION, Victor Mollo	P700	1.25
Win at backgammon? WINNING BACKGAMMON, Lawrence	P860	1.95
Make up a TV commercial? DOWN THE TUBE, Galanoy	P091	1.25
Become clairvoyant? HOW TO DEVELOP YOUR ESP, Smith	P246	1.25
Outwit today's stock market? PANICS & CRASHES, Schultz	P516	1.50

YOU CAN ORDER ANY OF THESE BOOKS RIGHT HERE: Please add 25¢ per book for postage and handling up to $1.00—free thereafter

Pinnacle Books
275 Madison Avenue
New York, N.Y. 10016

_____Check here if you wish our free catalog

PB-25

ALL NEW DYNAMITE SERIES
THE DESTROYER
by Richard Sapir & Warren Murphy

CURE, the world's most secret crime-fighting organization created the perfect weapon —Remo Williams—man programmed to become a cold, calculating death machine. The super man of the 70s!

Order		Title	Book No.	Price
_____	# 1	Created, The Destroyer	P361	$1.25
_____	# 2	Death Check	P362	$1.25
_____	# 3	Chinese Puzzle	P363	$1.25
_____	# 4	Mafia Fix	P364	$1.25
_____	# 5	Dr. Quake	P365	$1.25
_____	# 6	Death Therapy	P366	$1.25
_____	# 7	Union Bust	P367	$1.25
_____	# 8	Summit Chase	P368	$1.25
_____	# 9	Murder's Shield	P369	$1.25
_____	#10	Terror Squad	P370	$1.25
_____	#11	Kill or Cure	P371	$1.25
_____	#12	Slave Safari	P372	$1.25
_____	#13	Acid Rock	P373	$1.25
_____	#14	Judgment Day	P303	$1.25
_____	#15	Murder Ward	P331	$1.25
_____	#16	Oil Slick	P418	$1.25
_____	#17	Last War Dance	P435	$1.25
_____	#18	Funny Money	P538	$1.25
_____	#19	Holy Terror	P640	$1.25
_____	#20	Assassins Play-Off	P708	$1.25
_____	#21	Deadly Seeds	P760	$1.25
_____	#22	Brain Drain	P805	$1.25
_____	#23	Child's Play	P842	$1.25
_____	#24	King's Curse	P879	$1.25

TO ORDER
Please check the space next to the book/s you want, send this order form together with your check or money order, include the price of the book/s and 25¢ for handling and mailing to:
PINNACLE BOOKS, INC. / P.O. BOX 4347
Grand Central Station / New York, N.Y. 10017

☐ CHECK HERE IF YOU WANT A FREE CATALOG

I have enclosed $_____ check_____ or money order_____ as payment in full. No C.O.D.'s.

Name_____

Address_____

City_____ State_____ Zip_____
(Please allow time for delivery.) PB-39

the Executioner

The gutsiest, most exciting hero in years. Imagine a guy at war with the Godfather and all his Mafioso relatives! He's rough, he's deadly, he's a law unto himself — nothing and nobody stops him!

THE EXECUTIONER SERIES by DON PENDLETON

Order		Title	Book #	Price
_____	# 1	WAR AGAINST THE MAFIA	P401	$1.25
_____	# 2	DEATH SQUAD	P402	$1.25
_____	# 3	BATTLE MASK	P403	$1.25
_____	# 4	MIAMI MASSACRE	P404	$1.25
_____	# 5	CONTINENTAL CONTRACT	P405	$1.25
_____	# 6	ASSAULT ON SOHO	P406	$1.25
_____	# 7	NIGHTMARE IN NEW YORK	P407	$1.25
_____	# 8	CHICAGO WIPEOUT	P408	$1.25
_____	# 9	VEGAS VENDETTA	P409	$1.25
_____	#10	CARIBBEAN KILL	P410	$1.25
_____	#11	CALIFORNIA HIT	P411	$1.25
_____	#12	BOSTON BLITZ	P412	$1.25
_____	#13	WASHINGTON I.O.U.	P413	$1.25
_____	#14	SAN DIEGO SIEGE	P414	$1.25
_____	#15	PANIC IN PHILLY	P415	$1.25
_____	#16	SICILIAN SLAUGHTER	P552	$1.25
_____	#17	JERSEY GUNS	P328	$1.25
_____	#18	TEXAS STORM	P353	$1.25
_____	#19	DETROIT DEATHWATCH	P419	$1.25
_____	#20	NEW ORLEANS KNOCKOUT	P475	$1.25
_____	#21	FIREBASE SEATTLE	P499	$1.25
_____	#22	HAWAIIAN HELLGROUND	P625	$1.25
_____	#23	ST. LOUIS SHOWDOWN	P687	$1.25
_____	#24	CANADIAN CRISIS	P779	$1.25
_____	#25	COLORADO KILL-ZONE	P824	$1.25
_____	#26	ACAPULCO RAMPAGE	P868	$1.25

and more to come . . .

TO ORDER

Please check the space next to the book/s you want, send this order form together with your check or money order, include the price of the book/s and 25¢ for handling and mailing to:

PINNACLE BOOKS, INC. / P.O. Box 4347
Grand Central Station / New York, N.Y. 10017

☐ CHECK HERE IF YOU WANT A FREE CATALOG

I have enclosed $_____ check _____ or money order _____ as payment in full. No C.O.D.'s.

Name _____

Address _____

City _____ State _____ Zip _____

(Please allow time for delivery)

PB-38

Violence is a man! His name is Edge...

The bloodiest action-series ever published, with a hero who is the meanest, most vicious killer the West has ever seen.

**It's sharp —
It's hard —
It's EDGE**

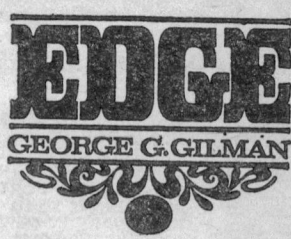

EDGE

GEORGE G. GILMAN

Order	#	Title	Book #	Price
___	#1	THE LONER	P596	$1.25
___	#2	TEN GRAND	P703	$1.25
___	#3	APACHE DEATH	P667	$1.25
___	#4	KILLER'S BREED	P597	$1.25
___	#5	BLOOD ON SILVER	P598	$1.25
___	#6	RED RIVER	P668	$1.25
___	#7	CALIFORNIA KILL	P599	$1.25
___	#8	HELL'S SEVEN	P750	$1.25
___	#9	BLOODY SUMMER	P293	.95
___	#10	BLACK VENGEANCE	P333	.95
___	#11	SIOUX UPRISING	P600	$1.25
___	#12	DEATH'S BOUNTY	P669	$1.25
___	#13	THE HATED	P560	$1.25
___	#14	TIGER'S GOLD	P624	$1.25
___	#15	PARADISE LOSES	P672	$1.25
___	#16	THE FINAL SHOT	P727	$1.25

AND MORE TO COME . . .

TO ORDER
Please check the space next to the book/s you want, send this order form together with your check or money order, include the price of the book/s and 25¢ for handling and mailing to:

PINNACLE BOOKS, INC. / P.O. BOX 4347
Grand Central Station / New York, N.Y. 10017
☐ CHECK HERE IF YOU WANT A FREE CATALOG
I have enclosed $_____ check_____ or money order_____ as payment in full. No C.O.D.'s.

Name_____

Address_____

City_____ State_____ Zip_____
(Please allow time for delivery.)

PN-59

IT'S ALWAYS ACTION WITH BLADE

HEROIC FANTASY SERIES
by Jeffrey Lord

The continuing saga of a modern man's exploits in the hitherto uncharted realm of worlds beyond our knowledge. Richard Blade is everyman and at the same time, a mighty and intrepid warrior. In the best tradition of America's most popular fictional heroes—giants such as Tarzan, Doc Savage and Conan—

		Title	Book #	Price
	#1	THE BRONZE AXE	P201	$ .95
	#2	THE JADE WARRIOR	P593	$1.25
	#3	JEWEL OF THARN	P203	$ .95
	#4	SLAVE OF SARMA	P204	$ .95
	#5	LIBERATOR OF JEDD	P205	$ .95
	#6	MONSTER OF THE MAZE	P206	$ .95
	#7	PEARL OF PATMOS	P767	$1.25
	#8	UNDYING WORLD	P208	$ .95
	#9	KINGDOM OF ROYTH	P295	$ .95
	#10	ICE DRAGON	P768	$1.25
	#11	DIMENSION OF DREAMS	P474	$1.25
	#12	KING OF ZUNGA	P523	$1.25
	#13	THE GOLDEN STEED	P559	$1.25
	#14	THE TEMPLES OF AYOCAN	P623	$1.25
	#15	THE TOWERS OF MELNON	P688	$1.25
	#16	THE CRYSTAL SEAS	P780	$1.25
	#17	THE MOUNTAINS OF BREGA	P812	$1.25
	#18	WARLORDS OF GAIKON	P822	$1.25
	#19	LOOTERS OF THARN	P855	$1.25
	#20	GUARDIANS OF THE CORAL THRONE	P881	$1.25

TO ORDER

Please check the space next to the books/s you want, send this order form together with your check or money order, include the price of the book/s and 25¢ for handling and mailing to:
PINNACLE BOOKS, INC. / P.O. Box 4347
Grand Central Station / New York, N.Y. 10017

☐ CHECK HERE IF YOU WANT A FREE CATALOG

I have enclosed $_____ check_____ or money order_____ as payment in full. No C.O.D.'s.

Name_____

Address_____

City_____ State_____ Zip_____

(Please allow time for delivery)   PB-35

THE PENETRATOR

by Lionel Derrick

Mark Hardin. Discharged from the army, after service in Vietnam. His military career was over. But *his* war was just beginning. His reason for living and reason for dying became the same—to stamp out crime and corruption wherever he finds it. He is deadly; he is unpredictable; and he is dedicated. He is The Penetrator!

Read all of him in:

Order	#	Title	Book No.	Price
_____	# 1	THE TARGET IS H	P236	$ .95
_____	# 2	BLOOD ON THE STRIP	P237	$ .95
_____	# 3	CAPITOL HELL	P318	$ .95
_____	# 4	HIJACKING MANHATTAN	P338	$ .95
_____	# 5	MARDI GRAS MASSACRE	P378	$ .95
_____	# 6	TOKYO PURPLE	P434	$1.25
_____	# 7	BAJA BANDIDOS	P502	$1.25
_____	# 8	THE NORTHWEST CONTRACT	P540	$1.25
_____	# 9	DODGE CITY BOMBERS	P627	$1.25
_____	#10	THE HELLBOMB FLIGHT	P690	$1.25

TO ORDER

Please check the space next to the book/s you want, send this order form together with your check or money order, include the price of the book/s and 25¢ for handling and mailing, to:
PINNACLE BOOKS, INC. / P.O. Box 4347
Grand Central Station / New York, N.Y. 10017
☐ Check here if you want a free catalog.

I have enclosed $_____ check_____ or money order_____ as payment in full. No C.O.D.'s.

Name_____

Address_____

City_____ State_____ Zip_____
(Please allow time for delivery)

PB-40